OVER 15,000 WORDS

The Scholastic Dictionary of

SPELLING

Marvin Terban

SCHOLASTIC
REFERENCE

For Karen and Jennifer, because you really need this book

Book design: Nancy Sabato
Composition: Kevin Callahan
Illustrations: Harry Campbell

No part of this publication may be reproduced in whole or in part, or stored in a retrieval system, or transmitted in any form or by any means, electronic, mechanical, photocopying, recording, or otherwise, without written permission of the publisher. For further information regarding permissions, write to Scholastic Inc., 555 Broadway, New York, NY 10012.

ISBN 0-590-30698-7

12 11 10 9   0 1 2 3/0

Printed in the U.S.A.   09

First Scholastic paperback printing, April 1998

Someone writes something. Other people read and understand it. That's good communication.

Someone writes something. Other people have trouble reading it. They misunderstand. That's poor communication.

The trouble can be that the letters are too small or the ink is too light or the writing is too messy. But very often the trouble is the spelling.

When your spelling is bad, it will take more time and effort for people to understand what you are trying to say. Bad spelling is confusing and perplexing and befuddling and frustrating and annoying—and embarrassing to the writer. So it's really important to spell as many words as possible as correctly as possible. That way, you'll get your meaning across, avoid misunderstandings, and save yourself from embarrassment.

English is a very tricky language with many, many words. According to some word experts, French has about 100,000 words, Russian has 135,000, and German has 185,000. But English has over 600,000 words! English is made up of words from about 100 other languages, so no wonder English spelling is so full of exceptions, irregularities, peculiarities, and just plain confusing words. It's not your fault English words are so hard to spell—but you should try your best to spell them right, just the same.

This book will help a lot, so keep it nearby when you write.

HOW TO LOOK UP A WORD

Luckily, many words in English are spelled just about the way they sound. Since all the words in this book are listed in alphabetical order, the way the beginning of a word is spelled is very important. Finding a word will be easier if you can get the first few letters right.

Slowly say the word you're trying to spell. (Say the word aloud if you can.) Think about what the first letter might be. Turn to the section of this dictionary that lists words that begin with that letter. (Use the large letters printed in the top corners of the pages to help you flip to the right section quickly.) Next, think about the first syllable. How do you think that could be spelled?

GUIDE WORDS

If you think you know the first few letters of a word, check them against the guide words in large print at the tops of the pages. Ask yourself: Is the word I'm looking for between these two guide words according to its alphabetical order?

For example, let's say you have to spell *cranberry, corporal,* and *criticize.* The guide words at the top of one page are *counselor* and *crazy. Cranberry* will be on that page, but *corporal* will be on an earlier page and *criticize* will be on a later page. That's because in alphabetical order, the words go: *corporal, counselor, cranberry, crazy, criticize.*

SYLLABLES

This dictionary breaks words into syllables as they are pronounced. The accented syllable (the one you pronounce a little more strongly) is printed in **boldface** type.

Sometimes words are accented differently, depending on how they are used in a sentence. For example, the word *permit* is pronounced **per**•mit as a noun (Here's my fishing **per**mit) and per•**mit** as a verb (I can't per**mit** you to do that). In this book, you will find the part of speech (noun, verb, adjective) of these especially tricky words abbreviated in parentheses (n., v., adj.).

SCAN

Once you think you know the first few letters, sound out the rest of the word to try to figure out the rest of the letters. Even if you are not sure which letters come in the middle and at the end, you can still probably find the word if you get the beginning right and then scan the lists. Look quickly up and down the columns. Sometimes you'll be able to spot the word as your eye travels on the page.

Please note that this special spelling dictionary is different from other dictionaries. Other books put words together that are related. The plural of a noun will come right after the singular, and other forms of a verb will come right after the present tense. But this dictionary lists all words in strict alphabetical order. For instance, *ladies* (plural noun) comes before *lady* (singular noun), and *carried* (the past tense of the verb) comes before *carry* (the present tense). So make sure that you scan both up and down the lists.

CONFUSING SOUNDS

Suppose you look up a word the way it sounds to you and you can't find it. Here are some suggestions.

If the word begins with a consonant sound

The consonant sounds are usually spelled as you might expect them to be. But sometimes a consonant sound can be spelled more than one way at the beginning of a word:

The **f** sound can be spelled with **f** (**f**abulous **f**un) or **ph** (**ph**araoh, **ph**easant).

The hard **g** sound can be spelled with **g** (**g**ame, **g**arden) or with **gh** (**gh**etto, **gh**ost).

The **j** sound can be spelled with **j** (**j**am, **j**elly) or with **g** (**g**iant, **g**ym).

The **k** sound can be spelled with **k** (**k**arate, **k**itchen), with **c** (**c**at, **c**omb), or with **ch** (**ch**lorine, **ch**orus).

The **n** sound can be spelled with **n** (**n**aughty, **n**ice), with **kn** (**kn**ee, **kn**ife, **kn**ot), with **gn** (**gn**ash, **gn**ome), or with **pn** (**pn**eumonia, **pn**eumatic).

The **r** sound can be spelled with **r** (**r**ascal, **r**eceive, **r**igmarole), with **wr** (**wr**angle, **wr**ench, **wr**iggle), or with **rh** (**rh**inoceros, **rh**ubarb, **rh**ythm).

The **s** sound can be spelled with **s** (**s**arcastic, **s**ecretary), with **c** (**c**ement, **c**inema, **c**yclone), with **sc** (**sc**issors, **sc**enery, **sc**epter), or with **ps** (**ps**alm, **ps**ychiatrist).

The **t** sound can be spelled with **t** (**t**ackle, **t**oadstool) or with **pt** (**pt**erodactyl, **pt**omaine).

The **w** sound can be spelled with **w** (**w**izard, **w**obble) or with **wh** (**wh**ale, **wh**imper).

The **z** sound can be spelled, with **z** (**z**any, **z**ombie) or with **x** (**X**erox, **x**ylophone).

Blends

Two or three consonants sometimes work together to form one sound at the beginning of a word, such as **sc** in **sc**are or **str** in **str**ong. Say **strong** aloud slowly. Do you hear the blend of letters? **s**. . . **t**. . . **r**. . . ong.

Sometimes the blends can have tricky spellings at the beginning of a word:

The **sh** sound can be spelled with **sh** (**sh**ark, **sh**epherd, **sh**iver), with **s** (**s**urely, **s**ugary), or with **ch** (**ch**ef, **ch**amois, **ch**arade).

The **sk** sound can be spelled with **sk** (**sk**ateboard, **sk**edaddle, **sk**ull), with **sc** (**sc**alpel, **sc**arecrow), with **sch** (**sch**edule, **sch**olar), or with **squ** (**squ**are, **squ**irrel, **squ**irt).

The **kr** sound can be spelled with **kr** (**Kr**emlin, **kr**ypton), with **cr** (**cr**y, **cr**eep, **cr**ocodile), or with **chr** (**Chr**istmas, **chr**omosome).

Make sure to think about all the letters in the blend before you start to look for the word.

Silent letters

Sometimes there are letters that make no sound at all at the beginning of a word, but you still have to put them in to spell the word right.

The letter **p** may be silent when it's followed by an **s** (as in **ps**ychic or **ps**eudonym) or by a **t** (as in **pt**armigan or **pt**erodactyl).

When the consonants **gn**, **kn**, and **wr** are written together, the first letter is silent (as in **gn**at, **kn**ot, and **wr**ote).

H is sometimes silent (as in **h**erb and **h**onest). The sound of the word starts with the sound of the vowel that follows the **h**.

If the word begins with a vowel . . .

Vowels have these sounds:

- *a* can sound like the *a* in *apple, able, always, alone*
- *e* can sound like the *e* in *elephant, equal, effect*
- *i* can sound like the *i* in *inch* or *idea*
- *o* can sound like the *o* in *olive, ocean,* or *other*
- *u* can sound like the *u* in *up* or *unit*

Because many vowels can make the same sound, you may have to look in more than one place in the dictionary to find a tricky vowel.

WHAT ABOUT HOMOPHONES?

Sometimes words that sound alike can be spelled differently and have different meanings. For example, look at the words *they're, there,* and *their.* You might say: "They're there in their house." But how do you know how to spell each homophone when you write the sentence?

In this dictionary, homophones are treated in a special way. Suppose you look up the word *there.* After the word, you will find in parentheses: (sounds like "their" and "they're"). Next, the word *there* will be used in a sentence to show you its meaning. If that's not the meaning you want, you should move up the list to the word *their*. You will find another sample sentence. If that's still not the right choice, you have one more option. You can move down the list to *they're*. Soon you will have the exact spelling of each word you want to use.

Note: Some teachers call homophones "homonyms."

COMPOUNDS

When a word is made up of other words, it is often difficult to decide how to write it. Should the words be written as one word, as in *cheerleader*, or are they divided by a hyphen, as in *old-fashioned*, or are they separated by a space, as in *air force*? This book can show you quickly the way the word should be written.

MORE HELP

Many words follow regular spelling patterns and are not too tough to spell once you know the rules. You'll find "A Dozen and One Spelling Rules" (and a few exceptions) beginning on page 9.

But other words don't follow the regular rules or have really hard spellings. Over time, people have made up tricks to help them remember how to spell these difficult words. You'll find a list of "Memory Tricks" beginning on page 14.

Sometimes it's hard to look up a word in the dictionary because the beginning of the word is not spelled the way you would expect. Words like that are listed in the "Misspeller's Dictionary" beginning on page 212. Turn to this section when all else fails.

No one is born a great speller, but if you work at it, you can get better. Just remember that when you're not 100%, absolutely, positively sure how to spell a word, look it up!

A Dozen and One Spelling Rules

Here are some helpful rules.

ADDING SUFFIXES

1. Don't change the spelling of the root word when you add the suffix **-ly** to any word that doesn't end in **y.**

   Examples:
   sincere + ly = sincerely
   beautiful + ly = beautifully

   Exceptions:
   true + ly = truly
   whole + ly = wholly

2. Don't change the spelling of the root word when you add the suffix **-ness** to any word that does not end in the letter **y.**

   Examples:
   kind + ness = kindness
   rough + ness = roughness

3. Keep the silent **e** at the end of a word when you add a suffix that begins with a **consonant** (like -**m**ent, -**f**ul, and -**l**y).

   Examples:
   arrange + ment = arrang**e**ment
   peace + ful = peac**e**ful
   sincere + ly = sinc**e**rely

   Exceptions:
   acknowledg**e** + ment = acknowled**gm**ent

judge + ment = ju**dgm**ent
true + ly = tr**ul**y
whole + ly = who**ll**y

4. Drop the silent **e** at the end of a word when you add a suffix that begins with a **vowel** (such as **-ed, -ing, -ous, -ably, -al,** and **-y**).

Examples:
hope + ing = hoping
shine + y = shiny
fortune + ate = fortunate
dose + age = dosage
nature + al = natural
fame + ous = famous

Exceptions: notic**ea**ble and courag**eo**us

5. Double the final consonant when the word is just one syllable, the last two letters are **one vowel + one consonant,** and you add a suffix that begins with a vowel (such as **-ing, -ed, -er, -est, -al, -y,** etc.).

Examples:
swim, swi**mm**ing, swi**mm**er
drag, dra**gg**ing, dra**gg**ed
hot, ho**tt**er, ho**tt**est
rob, ro**bb**ing, ro**bb**er
flop, flo**pp**y, flo**pp**ing

6. Change the **y** to **i** before adding the suffix when you add the suffixes **-ness, -age,** or **-ly** to any word that ends in the letter **y.**

Examples:
busy + ness = business

lonely + ness = loneliness
marry + age = marriage
happy + ness = happiness
day + ly = daily

7. Add **ful** not **full** when you add the suffix **-ful** to any word.

Examples:
thought + ful = thoughtful
cheer + ful = cheerful

FORMING PLURALS

8. Just add **s** when a word ends with **o** and there's a **vowel** before the **o**.

Examples:
one rodeo, two rodeos
one radio, two radios

9. Add **es** when a word ends with **o** and there's a **consonant** before the **o**.

Examples:
one tomato, two tomatoes
one torpedo, two torpedoes

Exception: With words that end with **o** and have something to do with **music**, just add **s** to form their **plurals**:
alto, altos
solo, solos
piano, pianos

Note: With the following words, either plural is correct, but the first is preferred: tornados or tornadoes, mosquitos or mosquitoes, dominos or dominoes, halos or haloes, mottos or mottoes, zeros or zeroes.

10. Just add **s** when the word ends with the letter **y** and there is a **vowel** before the **y**.

Examples:
one boy, two boy**s**
one key, two key**s**

11. Change the **y** to **i** and add **es** when the word ends with the letter **y,** and there is a **consonant** before the **y**.

Examples:
one lady, two lad**ies**
one country, two countr**ies**

FORMING COMPOUNDS

12. Don't change the spelling of either word when you want to put **two words together** to form a new compound word.

Examples:
baby + sitter = baby-sitter
teen + age = teenage
shoe + lace = shoelace

If the first word ends with the same letter that the second word begins with, keep both letters in the middle of the new compound word.

Examples:
roo**m** + **m**ate = roo**mm**ate
nigh**t** + **t**ime = nigh**tt**ime

Exception: pas**t** + **t**ime = pastime

Note: Sometimes the compound word will be one word (example: **sandpaper**), two words (example: **high school**), or a word with a hyphen in the middle (example: **custom-made**).

There's no rule for this. If you're not sure which version of your compound word is correct, look it up.

AN OLD RHYME

13. **I** before **e** (or is it **e** before **i**?)

If you know a word has the letters **i** and **e** in it together, but you can't remember which comes first, recite this well-known poem:

I *before* **e**
Except after **c**
Or when sounded like **a**
As in neighbor *and* weigh

That rule will work for most words such as: **achievement, believe, brief, chief, die, grief, lie, pie, retrieve, tie, unwieldy, ceiling, conceit, conceited, conceive, deceit, deceive, perceive, receipt, receive, beige, eighty, freight, neigh, reign, reindeer, sleigh, veil, vein,** and **weight**.

Exceptions: Here are the words that do the *opposite* of the poem: **ancient, being, caffeine, codeine, counterfeit, deficient, efficient, either, financier, foreign, forfeit, heifer, height, heir, kaleidoscope, leisure, neither, protein, scientist, seismologist, seize, sheik, sleight, society, species, stein, sufficient, their, weird**.

Memory Tricks

Trying to spell some words can be very difficult. Sometimes it helps to know a trick or two. Here are some good memory tricks for more than 150 words that are often spelled wrong.

accident
car **c**rash + **dent** = a**cc**i**dent**.

accommodations
At the **clean**, **cute**, **marvelous motel**, the a**ccomm**odations are good.

acre
The cathedral is built on a **sacre**d **acre** of land.

address
ad + **dress** = **address**

advice
My adv**ice** is don't slip on the **ice**.

advise
I ad**vise** you not to catch your finger in the **vise**.

all right
All right is all wrong if it's not *two words*.

altar
The workman got **tar** on the church al**tar**.

alter
She had to al**ter** the **ter**rible gown.

altogether
The **alto** sings **alto**gether lovely songs.

amateur
I, an **amateur**, **am at Eur**ope's shores.

answer
Were you going to give the ans**wer**?

architect
The **arch**itect drew the **arch**.

arctic
The first **c** in arctic stands for **c**old.

arithmetic
I **met** my arith**met**ic teacher at the mall.

athlete
In the b**ath let e**very **athlete** soak tired muscles.

attendance
at + **ten** + **dance** = **attendance**

autumn
There are **m**any **n**ice events at the end of autu**mn**.

awful
Alligator **w**as **f**eeling **u**nhappy **l**ately. How **awful**!

baggage
Ba**ggage** is lu**ggage**.

balloon
A **ball**oon can be shaped like a **ball**.

banana
This ba**na**na is *triple* A quality.

bargain
You can **gain** a lot if you get a bar**gain**.

bazaar

You can **b**uy **a**ncient **z**ebras **and a**musing **r**abbits at a **bazaar**.

beautiful

My **beau** (boyfriend) called me **beau**tiful.

beggar

Did the **beggar beg** in front of the **gar**age?

beginning

The second **inning** is beg**inning**.

behavior

To hit someone with your **vio**lin is bad beha**vio**r.

believe

Don't be**lie**ve a **lie**.

bicycle

It's dangerous to ride a b**icy**cle on an **icy** road.

bookkeeper

This is the only word with three sets of double letters in a row: **oo kk ee**.

brake

For goodness s**ake**, step on the br**ake**!

break

"**Brea**k **brea**d" means to eat.

buoy

This b**uo**y warns ships of **u**nderwater **o**bstacles.

burglar

A bur**glar** doesn't like the **glar**e of a light.

business

bus + **in** + **ess** = **business**

capital
A is the first capit**al** letter of the **al**phabet.

capitol
The dome on the capitol building is round like the **o** in capit**o**l.

captain
On your **cap** there is a s**tain**, **captain**.

cemetery
Do you scream "**e** . . .**c** . . .**c!**" when you go past a **cemetery**?

cereal
This ce**real** is made of **real** oats.

chief
"**Hi**," said the c**hi**ef.

chocolate
I was **late**, so I ate all the choco**late**.

choose
Why did the m**oose** ch**oose** a g**oose** with l**oose** feathers?

college
There's a **leg** in col**leg**e.

colonel
The **lone** co**lone**l won the battle.

committee
Marvelous **M**ike, **T**errific **T**om, and **E**legant **E**ve are on the co**mmittee**.

compliment
I am grateful for your nice compl**i**ment.

Connecticut
Connect me to **Connect**icut, please.

conscience
In **science** class, we are studying a frog's con**science**.

corps
P.S. The last two letters in cor**ps** are silent.

correspondence
In his **den**, he read his correspon**den**ce.

criticize
Don't critic**ize** the pr**ize**.

dessert
I like **s**omething **s**weet for de**ss**ert.

doctor
If you follow the doct**or**'s **or**ders, you'll get well.

dyeing
Don't leave the **dye in** too long when you're **dyein**g your hair.

eighth
Eighth begins with **eight**.

exaggerate
Good **g**rief! There's a **rat** in exa**ggerat**e!

existence
There **is** a **ten** in ex**isten**ce.

extraordinary
This is more than ordinary. It's **extra**ordinary.

February
Cold people say "**br**" in Fe**br**uary.

fiend
Let's put an **end** to this fi**end**.

flammable
Many **m**atches are fla**mm**able.

foreign
The **foreign** man needed a room **for eig**ht **n**ights.

forth
March **fort**h from the **fort**.

forty
The **fort** held out for **fort**y days.

fourth
Four is the **four**th number.

gallon
All I need is a g**all**on.

gnarled
Gee, this is a **nar**row **led**ge to climb with **gnarled** hands.
(Note: The "g" in **gnarled** is silent.)

governor
The **governor** will **govern or** we won't vote for him.

grammar
Don't **mar** (spoil) your writing with bad gram**mar**.

guarantee
The **guar**d, **an** old friend, will **tee** off at three o'clock.

hangar
A han**gar** is like a **gar**age for planes.

hanger
Do you feel **anger** when your clothes fall off your **h**anger?

hear

With my **ear** I h**ear**.

here, there, where

All three words end with "**ere**."

immigrant

Many **m**illions of people were **grant**ed the right to be i**mmigrant**s.

inoculation

An **in**oculation is when the doctor sticks the needle **in**.

interrupt

It's **r**eally **r**ude to inte**rr**upt someone.

it's

If you can substitute "**it is**," then it's "**it's**."

language

This langu**age** has been spoken since a long-ago **age.**

library

It's **rar**e not to find a good book in the lib**rar**y.

license

Do **lice** have a **lice**nse to live here?

loose, noose, goose

Take the n**oose** off the neck of the l**oose** g**oose**.

lose

Did the clown l**ose** his rubber n**ose**?

maintenance

The **main** thing is for **ten** of the **mainten**ance men to fix the leak.

mantel

Can the **man** **tele**phone from the **mantel**?

marriage
If I **marr**y, will **I age** faster after my **marriage**?

mathematics
Ma, the mat has **mathemat**ics written on it.

medieval
Did many people **die** in me**die**val times?

mileage
mile + **age** = **mileage**

miscellaneous
In his **cell**, the prisoner found mis**cell**aneous things.

misspell
Miss Pell would **misspell** everything!

naive
An**na, I've** been so **naive.**

niece
This p**iece** belongs to my n**iece.**

occasion
This special o**cc**a**s**ion **c**alls for **c**oconut **c**ustard and **s**oda.

occur
When did the **c**ar **c**rash o**cc**ur?

often
She gives the right answer nine out **of ten** times, which is pretty **often**.

ough words
I'm **tough** and thor**ough**, and I **fough**t thr**ough** the **rough** storm, and I **though**t I had **sough**t and **bough**t and br**ough**t enough **cough** syrup for the whole winter.

pageant

page + **ant** = **pageant**

pajamas

Did **Pa jam** his **pajam**as in the drawer?

parallel

The two **l**'s in para**ll**el are parallel lines.

pavilion

There's a **lion** in the pavi**lion**!

peace

There's pe**ace** in this pl**ace**.

physician

What is the **ph**ysician's **ph**one number?

piece

Please cut me a **pie**ce of **pie**.

playwright

The play**wr**ight **wr**ote a beautiful play.

porpoise

Is that n**oise** coming from the porp**oise**?

potatoes

Her **toes** looked like little pota**toes**.

prairie

The **air** on the pr**air**ie is fresh and clean.

prey

Predators **pre**y on other animals.

principal

The princi**pal** of the school is your **pal**.

principle
A princip**le** is a ru**le** of life.

professor
A pro**fess**or is **f**requently **s**omeone **s**mart.

pronunciation
The **nun** has clear pro**nun**ciation.

purchase
She opened her **pur**se to make her **pur**chase.

quiet
Try a qu**iet** d**iet**.

quite
You have qu**ite** an appet**ite**.

raspberry
G**rasp** the **rasp**berry and squeeze it.

realize
I **real**ized the diamond was **real**.

receipt
Shh! The **p** is silent in recei**p**t.

recipe
The rec**ipe** calls for **ripe** vegetables.

resistance
Sis has a **tan** in re**sistan**ce.

restaurant
Rest, dinos**aur** and **ant**, at this **restaurant**.

rhinoceros
The **rh**inoceros writes **rh**ymes.

ridiculous

He had to get **rid** of his **rid**iculous hat.

role

He has a **role** in the wh**ole** play.

roll

I tried to r**oll** the tr**oll** over the kn**oll**.

safety

Be **safe**. Practice **safe**ty.

scene

I was **sc**ared by that **sc**ene in the movie.

scheme

He hatched a **sch**eme to get out of **sch**ool.

scissors

With **sc**issors, he cut the hair off his **sc**alp.

secretary

That **secret**ary has a **secret** she's not telling.
There's **tar** on the secre**tar**y's shoes.

separate

There's **a rat** in sep**arat**e.

shriek

"D**ie**!" he shr**ie**ked.

skiing

Keep both your *i*'s open when sk**ii**ng.

soldier

The sol**die**r did not **die**.

squeak
Does the mouse sp**eak** with a squ**eak**?

stationary
The **a** in station**a**ry stands for st**a**y.

stationery
The **e** in station**e**ry stands for **e**nvelope.

steal
Did he st**eal** the r**eal** treasure?

steel
The wh**eel** is made of st**eel**.

surgeon
I will **urge on** the s**urgeon** to perform the operation.

sword
Take my **word** for it, this s**word** is sharp.

than
I like this pl**an** better th**an** D**an**'s plan.

their, there, they're
All three begin with "**the**."

thief
A th**ief** will **lie**.

tomorrow
Tom, there will be no s**orrow tomorrow**.

tongue
An elephant's **tongue** weighs a **ton**, and he uses it to ar**gue**.

tragedy

Old **age** is not a **trage**dy.

trouble

This is not **our** trouble; it's y**our** trou**ble**.

vacuum

Make sure to vac**uu**m **up** **u**nder the sofa.

villain

The **villain** lives in a **villa in** the country.

weather

In rainy **weather**, **we** look **at her** picture.

Wednesday

She will **wed** next **Wed**nesday.

which

Wh**ich** **rich** person donated the money?

witch

The w**itch** scratched her **itch**.

yacht

This is the b**ach**elor's y**ach**t.

yolk

The gentle f**olk** eat the y**olk**.

aard•vark
ab•a•cus
ab•a•lo•ne
a•ban•don
a•bate
a•bate•ment
a•bat•ing
ab•bey
ab•bot
ab•bre•vi•ate
ab•bre•vi•at•ing
ab•bre•vi•a•tion
ab•di•cate
ab•di•cat•ing
ab•di•ca•tion
ab•do•men
ab•dom•i•nal
ab•duct
ab•duc•tion
ab•duc•tor
ab•hor•rent
a•bide
a•bid•ing
a•bil•i•ties
a•bil•i•ty
a•blaze
a•ble
a•ble-bod•ied
a•bly
ab•nor•mal
ab•nor•mal•i•ty
a•board

a•bode
a•bol•ish
a•bo•li•tion
a•bo•li•tion•ist
a•bom•i•na•ble
a•bom•i•na•bly
ab•o•rig•i•nal
Ab•o•rig•i•ne
a•bound
a•bout
a•bove
a•bove•board
ab•ra•ca•dab•ra
a•brade
a•bra•sion
ab•ra•sive
a•breast
a•bridge
a•bridged

ablaze

a•bridg•ing
a•bridg•ment
a•broad
a•brupt
a•brupt•ly
ab•scess
ab•sence
ab•sent
ab•sent-mind•ed
ab•so•lute
ab•so•lute•ly
ab•so•lu•tion
ab•solve
ab•so•lu•tion
ab•sorb
ab•sorb•ent
ab•sorp•tion
ab•stain
ab•sten•tion
ab•sti•nence
ab•stract (adj. and n.)
ab•stract (v.)
ab•strac•tion
ab•surd
ab•sur•di•ties
ab•sur•di•ty
a•bun•dance
a•bun•dant
a•buse
a•bus•ing
a•bu•sive
a•byss

ac•a•**dem**•ic
ac•a•**dem**•i•cal•ly
a•**cad**•e•mies
a•**cad**•e•my
a cap•**pel**•la
ac•**cel**•er•ate
ac•**cel**•er•at•ing
ac•**cel**•er•**a**•tion
ac•**cel**•er•**a**•tor
ac•cent
ac•**cen**•tu•ate
ac•**cept** (sounds like
   "except")

   *I accept your kind
   offer.*

ac•cept•a•**bil**•i•ty
ac•**cept**•a•ble
ac•**cept**•ance
ac•cess
ac•**ces**•si•ble
ac•**ces**•so•ry
ac•ci•dent
ac•ci•**den**•tal
ac•ci•**den**•tal•ly
ac•**claim**
ac•cla•**ma**•tion
ac•**com**•mo•date
ac•com•mo•**dat**•ing
ac•com•mo•**da**•tion
ac•**com**•pa•nied
ac•**com**•pa•nies
ac•**com**•pa•ni•ment
ac•**com**•pa•nist
ac•**com**•pa•ny

ac•**com**•plice
ac•**com**•plish
ac•**com**•plish•ment
ac•**cord**
ac•**cor**•dance
ac•**cor**•di•on
ac•**cor**•di•on•ist
ac•**cost**
ac•**count**
ac•count•a•**bil**•i•ty
ac•**count**•a•ble
ac•**count**•ant
ac•**cu**•mu•late
ac•**cu**•mu•lat•ing
ac•cu•mu•**la**•tion
ac•cu•ra•cy
ac•cu•rate
ac•cu•**sa**•tion
ac•**cuse**
ac•**cus**•ing
ac•**cus**•tomed
ace
ac•e•tate
ac•e•tone
a•**cet**•y•lene
ache
a•**chieve**
a•**chieve**•ment
a•**chiev**•ing
A•**chil**•les
ach•ing
ac•id
a•**cid**•ic
a•**cid**•i•ty

ac•**knowl**•edge
ac•**knowl**•edg•ing
ac•**knowl**•edg•ment
ac•ne
a•corn
a•**cou**•stic
a•**cou**•stics
ac•**quain**•tance
ac•**quire**
ac•**quir**•ing
ac•**quit**
ac•**quit**•tal
ac•**quit**•ted
a•cre
a•cre•age
ac•ro•bat
ac•ro•**bat**•ics
ac•ro•nym
a•**crop**•o•lis
a•**cross**
a•**cryl**•ic
act
act•ing
ac•tion
ac•ti•vate
ac•ti•vat•ing
ac•ti•**va**•tion
ac•ti•va•tor
ac•tive
ac•**tiv**•i•ty
ac•tor
ac•tress
ac•tu•al
ac•tu•**al**•i•ty

ac•tu•al•ly
ac•u•punc•ture
a•**cute**
ad
ad•age
a•**da**•gi•o
ad•a•mant
a•**dapt**
a•dapt•a•**bil**•i•ty
a•**dapt**•a•ble
ad•ap•ta•tion
a•**dapt**•er
(*or* a•**dap**•tor)
a•**dap**•tive
add

(**add**)

ad•dend
ad•**den**•dum
ad•dict
ad•**dic**•tion
ad•**dic**•tive
ad•**di**•tion
ad•**di**•tion•al

ad•**di**•tive
ad•**dress**
also pronounced
ad•dress
ad•dress•**ee**
ad•e•noid
ad•e•qua•cy
ad•e•quate
ad•**here**
ad•**he**•sion
ad•**he**•sive
a•**dieu**
a•di•**os**
ad•**ja**•cent
ad•jec•tive
ad•**journ**
ad•**journ**•ment
ad•**just**
ad•**just**•a•ble
ad•**just**•ment
ad lib
ad•**min**•is•ter
ad•**min**•is•tra•tor
ad•mi•ra•ble
ad•mi•ral
ad•**mire**
ad•**mir**•ing
ad•**mis**•si•ble
ad•**mis**•sion
ad•**mit**
ad•**mit**•tance
ad•**mit**•ted
ad•**mit**•ting
ad•**mon**•ish

ad•mo•**ni**•tion
a•**do**•be
ad•o•**les**•cence
ad•o•**les**•cent
a•**dopt**
a•**dop**•tion
a•**dor**•a•ble
ad•o•**ra**•tion
a•**dore**
a•**dor**•ing
a•**dorn**
a•**dorned**
a•**dorn**•ment
ad•**ren**•a•lin
a•**drift**
a•**dult**
also pronounced
a•dult
a•**dult**•hood
ad•**vance**
ad•**vanc**•ing
ad•**van**•tage
ad•van•**ta**•geous
ad•vent
ad•**ven**•ture
ad•**ven**•tur•er
ad•**ven**•ture•some
ad•**ven**•tur•ous
ad•verb
ad•ver•sar•ies
ad•ver•sar•y
ad•**verse**
ad•**ver**•si•ties
ad•**ver**•si•ty

ad•ver•tise
ad•ver•**tise**•ment
  also pronounced
  ad•**ver**•tise•ment
ad•**vice**
ad•vis•a•**bil**•i•ty
ad•**vis**•a•ble
ad•**vise**
ad•**vis**•er (or ad•**vis**•or)
ad•vo•cate (v.)
ad•vo•**cate** (n.)
ad•vo•cat•ing
aer•i•al
aer•i•al•ist
aer•o•**bat**•ics
aer•**o**•bics
aer•o•dy•**nam**•ic
aer•o•**nau**•ti•cal
aer•o•**nau**•tics
aer•o•sol
aer•o•space
Ae•sop
af•fa•ble
af•**fair**
af•**fect** (may sound like
  "effect")
  The weather may
  affect our plans.
af•**fect**•ed
af•**fec**•tion
af•**fec**•tion•ate
af•**fec**•tive
af•**fil**•i•ate
af•**fil**•i•at•ing

af•fil•i•**a**•tion
af•**firm**
af•fir•**ma**•tion
af•**firm**•a•tive
af•**flu**•ence
af•**flu**•ent
af•**ford**
af•**ford**•a•ble
af•ghan
a•**float**

afloat

a•**fraid**
a•**fresh**
Af•ri•can A•**mer**•i•can
Af•ro
aft
af•ter
af•ter•math
af•ter•**noon**
af•ter•thought
af•ter•ward (or

af•ter•wards)
a•**gain**
a•**gainst**
ag•ate
age
aged
  also pronounced
  a•ged
age•ism
age•less
a•**gen**•cy
a•**gen**•da
a•**gent**
ag•gra•vate
ag•gra•vat•ing
ag•gra•**va**•tion
ag•gre•gate
ag•**gres**•sion
ag•**gres**•sive
a•**ghast**
ag•ile
a•**gil**•i•ty
ag•ing
ag•i•tate
ag•i•tat•ing
ag•i•**ta**•tion
a•**go**
ag•o•nies
ag•o•nize
ag•o•ny
a•**gree**
a•**gree**•a•ble
a•**greed**
a•**gree**•ment

ag•ri•**cul**•tur•al
ag•ri•cul•ture
a•**ground**
a•**head**
a•**hoy**
aid (sounds like "aide")
   *They gave aid to
   the refugees.*
aide (sounds like "aid")
   *The aide works closely
   with the doctor.*
AIDS
ai•**ki**•do
ail•ment
aim
aim•less
air (sounds like "heir")
   Birds fly in the air.
air con•**di**•tion•er
air con•**di**•tion•ing
air•craft
air•craft **car**•ri•er
air•field
air force
air•line
air•mail
air•plane
air•port
air raid
air•ship
air•sick
air•sick•ness
air•strip
air•tight

air•wor•thy
air•y
aisle (sounds like "I'll"
   and "isle")
   *The bride walked
   down the aisle.*
a•**jar**
a•**kim**•bo
a•**kin**
Al•a•**bam**•a
a•la•bas•ter
a la **carte**
a la **mode**
a•**larm**
a•**las**
A•**las**•ka
al•ba•tross
al•**bi**•no
al•bum
al•che•mist
al•che•my
al•co•hol
al•co•**hol**•ic
al•co•hol•ism
al•cove
al•der
ale
a•**lert**
al•**fal**•fa
al•gae
al•ge•bra
al•ge•**bra**•ic
a•li•as
al•i•bi

al•ien
al•ien•**a**•tion
a•**lign**
a•**lign**•ment
a•**like**
al•i•**men**•ta•ry
   ca•**nal**
al•i•mo•ny
a•**live**
al•ka•li
al•ka•line
all (sounds like
   "awl")
   We ate all the food.
Al•lah
al•**lay**
al•le•**ga**•tion
al•**lege**
al•**leged**
al•**leg**•ed•ly
al•**le**•giance
al•le•**gor**•i•cal
al•le•go•ry
al•**ler**•gic
al•**le**•vi•ate
al•**le**•vi•at•ing
al•ley
al•**li**•ance
al•lied
   also pronounced
   al•**lied**
al•lies
al•li•ga•tor
al•lit•er•**a**•tion

al•**lot** (sounds like
  "a lot")
  *How much time did
  we allot for math?*
al•**lot**•ment
al•**lot**•ted
al•**low**
al•**low**•a•ble
al•**low**•ance
al•**low**•ed
al•loy
all right
al•**lude** (sounds like
  "elude")
  *I allude to the
  president's speech
  where the idea was
  mentioned.*
al•**lud**•ing
al•ly
al•ma **ma**•ter
al•ma•nac
al•**might**•y
al•mond
al•most
al•oe
a•**loft**
a•**lo**•ha
a•**lone**
a•**long**
a•**long**•side
a•**loof**
a•**loof**•ness
a lot (sounds like "allot")
  She likes fudge a lot.

a•**loud**
al•**pac**•a
al•pha•bet
al•pha•**bet**•i•cal
al•pha•bet•ize
al•**read**•y
al•so
al•tar (sounds like
  "alter")
  I prayed at the altar.
al•ter (sounds like
  "altar")
  *I'm going to alter
  my dress.*
al•ter•**a**•tion
al•ter•**ca**•tion
al•ter **e**•go
al•ter•nate
al•ter•nat•ing
al•**ter**•na•tive
al•**though**
al•**tim**•e•ter
al•ti•tude
al•to
al•to•**geth**•er
al•tos
a•**lu**•mi•num
a•**lum**•na (f. sing.)
a•**lum**•nae (f. pl.)
a•**lum**•ni (m. pl.)
a•**lum**•nus (m. sing.)
al•ways
am
am•a•teur

am•a•**teur**•ish
a•**maze**
a•**maze**•ment
a•**maz**•ing
am•**bas**•sa•dor
am•ber
am•bi•dex•**ter**•i•ty
am•bi•**dex**•trous
am•bi•**gu**•i•ty
am•**big**•u•ous
am•**bi**•tion
am•**bi**•tious
am•**biv**•a•lence
am•**biv**•a•lent
am•ble
am•bling
am•bu•lance

(**ambulance**)

am•bu•la•to•ry
am•bush
a•**men**
a•**mend**

a•**mend**•ment
A•**mer**•i•ca
A•**mer**•i•can
A•**mer**•i•can **In**•di•an
am•e•thyst
a•mi•a•**bil**•i•ty
a•mi•a•ble
a•mi•a•bly
a•**mi**•go
Am•ish
am•**mo**•nia
am•mu•**ni**•tion
am•**ne**•sia
am•nes•ty
a•**moe**•ba (sing.)
a•**moe**•bae (pl.)
a•**moe**•bas (pl.)
a•**mong**
a•**mongst**
a•**mount**
amp
am•**phi**•bi•an
am•**phib**•i•ous
am•phi•the•a•ter
am•ple
am•pli•fi•**ca**•tion
am•pli•fied
am•pli•fi•er
am•pli•fies
am•pli•fy
am•pli•fy•ing
am•ply
am•pu•tate
am•pu•tat•ing

am•pu•**ta**•tion
am•pu•**tee**
a•**muse**
a•**muse**•ment
a•**mus**•ing
an
an•a•**con**•da
an•a•gram
an•a•log
a•**nal**•y•ses
a•**nal**•y•sis
an•a•lyze
an•a•lyz•ing
an•a•**tom**•i•cal
a•**nat**•o•my
an•ces•tor
an•ces•try
an•chor
an•cho•vies
an•cho•vy
also pronounced
an•**cho**•vy
an•cient
and
an•droid
an•ec•dote
a•**ne**•mi•a
a•**ne**•mic
a•**nem**•o•ne
an•es•**the**•sia
an•es•**thet**•ic
a•**nes**•the•tist
a•**nes**•the•tize
a•**new**

an•gel (often confused
with "angle")
An angel has wings.
an•ger
an•gle (often confused
with "angel")
*This triangle has a
right angle.*
an•**go**•ra
an•gri•ly
an•gry
an•guish
an•gu•lar
an•i•mal
an•i•mat•ed
an•i•mat•ing
an•i•**ma**•tion
an•i•**mos**•i•ty
an•kle
an•nex
also pronounced
an•**nex**
an•**ni**•hi•late
an•ni•hi•**la**•tion
an•**ni**•hi•la•tor
an•ni•**ver**•sa•ries
an•ni•**ver**•sa•ry
an•no•tate
an•no•**ta**•tion
an•**nounce**
an•**nounce**•ment
an•**nounc**•er
an•**nounc**•ing
an•**noy**

an•**noy**•ance
an•nu•al
an•**nul**
an•**nulled**
an•**nul**•ling
an•**nul**•ment
a•**noint**
an•o•**nym**•i•ty
a•**non**•y•mous
an•o•rak
an•o•**rex**•ic
an•**oth**•er
an•swer
an•swer•a•ble
ant (sounds like
  "aunt")
  *An ant crawled into
  our picnic.*
an•**tag**•o•nism
an•**tag**•o•nist
an•tag•o•**nis**•tic
an•**tag**•o•nize
an•**tag**•o•niz•ing
Ant•**arc**•tic
Ant•**arc**•ti•ca
ant•eat•er
an•te•**ced**•ent
an•te•lope
an•**ten**•na
an•them
an•ther
an•**thol**•o•gy
an•thra•cite
an•thro•**pol**•o•gist

an•thro•**pol**•o•gy
an•ti•bi•**ot**•ic
an•ti•bod•y
an•**tic**•i•pate
an•**tic**•i•pat•ing
an•**tic**•i•pa•tion
an•ti•**cli**•max
an•ti•dote
an•ti•freeze
an•ti•**his**•ta•mine
an•ti•**pas**•to
an•ti•**per**•spi•rant
an•**tique**
an•ti-**Sem**•i•tism
an•ti•**sep**•tic
an•ti•**so**•cial
an•ti•**tox**•in
an•ti•**trust**
ant•ler
an•to•nym
anx•**i**•e•ty
anx•ious
an•y
an•y•bod•y
an•y•how
an•y•**more**
an•y•one
an•y•place
an•y•thing
an•y•time
an•y•way
an•y•where
a•**or**•ta
A•**pach**•e

a•**part**
a•**part**•heid
a•**part**•ment
ap•a•**thet**•ic
ap•a•thy
ape
ap•er•ture
a•pex
a•**piece**
a•pol•o•**get**•ic
a•**pol**•o•gies
a•**pol**•o•gize
a•**pol**•o•giz•ing
a•**pol**•o•gy
a•**pos**•tle
a•**pos**•tro•phe
ap•**pall**•ing
ap•pa•**rat**•us
ap•**par**•el
ap•**par**•ent
ap•pa•**ri**•tion
ap•**peal**
ap•**peal**•ing
ap•**pear**
ap•**pear**•ance
ap•**pease**
ap•**pen**•di•ces
ap•pen•di•**ci**•tis
ap•**pen**•dix
ap•**pen**•dix•es
ap•pe•tite
ap•pe•tiz•er
ap•pe•tiz•ing
ap•**plaud**

ap•**plaud**•ed
ap•**plause**
ap•ple
ap•ple•sauce
ap•**pli**•ance
ap•pli•cant
ap•pli•**ca**•tion
ap•**ply**
ap•**point**
ap•**point**•ment
ap•po•**si**•tion
ap•**prais**•al
ap•**praise**
ap•**pre**•ci•ate
ap•**pre**•ci•at•ing
ap•**pre**•ci•a•tive
ap•pre•**hend**
ap•pre•**hen**•sive
ap•**pren**•tice
ap•**pren**•tice•ship
ap•**proach**
ap•**proach**•a•ble
ap•**pro**•pri•ate
ap•**prove**
ap•**prov**•ing
ap•**prox**•i•mate
ap•prox•i•**ma**•tion
a•pri•cot
A•pril
a•pron
apt
ap•ti•tude
Aq•ua-Lung
aq•ua•ma•**rine**

a•**quar**•i•um
a•**quat**•ic
aq•ue•duct
A•**ra**•bi•a
Ar•a•bic
ar•a•ble
ar•bi•trar•y
ar•bi•trate
ar•bi•**trat**•ing
ar•bi•**tra**•tion
ar•bi•**tra**•tor
ar•bor
arc
ar•**cade**
arch
ar•chae•**o**•lo•gy (*or*
  ar•che•**ol**•o•gy)
ar•che•**ol**•o•gist
ar•che•o•**log**•i•cal
ar•**cha**•ic
arch•**bish**•op
arch•duke

(Aqua-Lung)

arch•e•ry
ar•chi•**pel**•a•go
ar•chi•tect
ar•chi•**tec**•tur•al
ar•chi•tec•ture
ar•chives
arch•way
arc•tic
Arc•tic **Cir**•cle
ar•dent
ar•dor
ar•du•ous
are
ar•e•a
a•**re**•na
aren't
Ar•gen•**ti**•na
ar•gue
ar•gu•ing
ar•gu•ment
ar•gu•**men**•ta•tive
a•ria
ar•id
a•**rise**
a•**ris**•en
a•**ris**•ing
ar•is•**toc**•ra•cy
a•**ris**•to•crat
a•ris•to•**crat**•ic
Ar•is•tot•le
a•**rith**•me•tic
Ar•i•**zo**•na
Ar•kan•sas
ark

arm
ar•**ma**•da
ar•ma•**dil**•lo
ar•ma•**dil**•los
arm•chair
Ar•**me**•ni•a
arm•ful
ar•mies
ar•mis•tice
ar•mor
ar•mor•ies
ar•mor•y
arm•pit
ar•my
a•**ro**•ma
a•ro•**mat**•ic
a•**round**
a•**rouse**
a•**rous**•ing
ar•**raign**
ar•**range**
ar•**ranged**
ar•**range**•ment
ar•**rang**•ing
ar•**rest**
ar•**ri**•val
ar•**rive**
ar•ro•gant
ar•row
ar•row•head
ar•se•nal
ar•se•nic
ar•son
art

ar•ter•ies
ar•te•ri•o•scle•**ro**•sis
ar•ter•y
ar•**thrit**•ic
ar•**thri**•tis
ar•thro•pod
ar•ti•choke
ar•tic•le
ar•**tic**•u•late
ar•**tic**•u•lat•ing
ar•ti•fact
ar•ti•**fi**•cial
ar•**til**•ler•y
ar•ti•san
art•ist
ar•**tis**•tic
art•ist•ry
as
as•**bes**•tos
as•**cend**
ash
a•**shamed**
ash•en
a•**shore**
A•sia
A•sian A•**mer**•i•can
a•**side**
ask
a•**skew**
a•**sleep**
as•**par**•a•gus
as•pect
as•pen
as•phalt

as•**phyx**•i•ate
as•**phyx**•i•at•ing
as•phyx•i•**a**•tion
as•pi•**ra**•tion
as•pi•rin
as•**sas**•sin
as•**sas**•si•nate
as•**sas**•si•nat•ing
as•**sas**•si•na•tion
as•**sault**
as•**sem**•ble
as•**sem**•blies
as•**sem**•bling
as•**sem**•bly
as•**sent**
as•**sert**
as•**ser**•tion
as•**ser**•tive
as•**sess**
as•**sess**•ment
as•**ses**•sor
as•set
as•**sign**
as•**sign**•ing
as•**sign**•ment
as•**sist**
as•**sist**•ance (sounds like "assistants")
I need your assistance to move this desk.
as•**sist**•ant
as•**sist**•ants (sounds like "assistance")
She has four assistants.

as•**so**•ci•ate
as•**so**•ci•at•ing
as•so•ci•**a**•tion
as•**sort**•ment
as•**sume**
as•**sum**•ing
as•**sump**•tion
as•**sur**•ance
as•**sure**
as•**sur**•ing
as•ter
as•ter•isk
as•ter•oid

asteroid

asth•ma
asth•**mat**•ic
a•**stig**•ma•tism
as•**ton**•ish
as•**ton**•ish•ment
as•**tound**
as•**tound**•ing
a•**stray**

a•**stride**
as•**trin**•gent
as•tro•dome
as•**trol**•o•ger
as•tro•**log**•i•cal
as•**trol**•o•gy
as•tro•naut
as•**tron**•o•mer
as•tro•**nom**•i•cal
as•**tron**•o•my
as•tro•**phys**•ics
as•**tute**
a•**sy**•lum
a•sym•**met**•ric
a•sym•**met**•ri•cal
a•**sym**•me•try
at
ate (sounds like"eight")
  I ate the whole cake
  myself.
a•the•ism
a•the•ist
Ath•ens
ath•lete
ath•**let**•ic
ath•**let**•i•cal•ly
ath•**let**•ics
At•**lan**•tic
at•las
at•mos•phere
at•mos•**pher**•ic
at•oll
at•om
a•**tom**•ic

a•**tone**
a•tri•um
a•**tro**•cious
a•**troc**•i•ty
at•**tach**
at•ta•**ché**
at•**tack**
at•**tain**
at•**tain**•ment
at•**tempt**
at•**tend**
at•**ten**•dance
at•**ten**•dant
at•**ten**•tion
at•**ten**•tive
at•**test**
at•tic
at•**tire**
at•ti•tude
at•**tor**•ney
at•**tract**
at•**trac**•tion
at•**trac**•tive
at•**trib**•ute (n.)
at•**trib**•ute (v.)
au•burn
auc•tion
auc•tion•**eer**
au•di•ble
au•di•bly
au•di•ence
au•di•o
au•di•o•tape
au•di•o•**vis**•u•al

au•**di**•tion

au•di•**to**•ri•um

au•di•to•ry

Au•du•bon

Au•gust

auld lang **syne**

aunt (sounds like "ant")

My aunt gave me a book.

au pair

au•ral (sounds like "oral")

Aural information comes in through your ear.

au•ri•cle

au•**ro**•ra bo•re•**al**•is

aus•**tere**

aus•**ter**•i•ty

au•**then**•tic

au•thor

au•thor•i•**tar**•i•an

au•**thor**•i•ta•tive

au•**thor**•i•ty

au•thor•i•**za**•tion

au•thor•ize

au•thor•iz•ing

au•thor•ship

au•**tis**•tic

au•to•bi•**og**•ra•pher

au•to•bi•o•**graph**•i•cal

au•to•bi•**og**•ra•phy

au•to•graph

au•to•**mat**•ic

au•to•**mat**•i•cal•ly

au•to•**ma**•tion

au•**tom**•a•ton

au•to•mo•bile

au•to•**mo**•tive

au•**ton**•o•mous

au•**ton**•o•my

au•top•sy

au•tumn

aux•**il**•ia•ry

a•vail•a•**bil**•i•ty

a•**vail**•a•ble

av•a•lanche

a•vant **garde**

a•**venge**

a•**veng**•ing

av•e•nue

av•er•age

a•**vert**

a•**vi**•ar•y

a•vi•**a**•tion

av•id

av•o•**ca**•do

av•o•**ca**•tion

a•**void**

a•**void**•ance

a•**vow**

a•**wait**

a•**wake**

a•**wak**•en

a•**ward**

a•**ware**

a•**ware**•ness

a•**way** (sounds like "aweigh")

She went away yesterday.

awe

a•**weigh** (sounds like "away")

Anchors aweigh!

awe•some

aw•ful

aw•ful•ly

awk•ward

awl (sounds like "all")

With an awl he made holes in the leather.

aw•ning

a•**wry**

ax (*or* **axe**)

ax•is

ax•le

aye

a•**za**•lea

Az•tec

az•ure

bab•ble
bab•bling
bab•ied
ba•bies
ba•**boon**
ba•**bush**•ka
ba•by
ba•by•hood
ba•by•ish
Bab•y•lon
ba•by-**sit**•ter
ba•by-**sit**•ting
bach•e•lor
bach•e•lor•hood
back
back•board
back•bone
back•**door**
back•drop
back•er
back•field
back•fire
back•gam•mon
back•ground
back•hand
back•hoe
back•lash
back•log
back•pack
back•side
back•slide
back•stage

back•stroke
back talk
back•ward
back•wa•ter
back•yard

(**bagpipes**)

ba•con
bac•**te**•ri•a
bac•**te**•ri•al
bac•te•ri•o•**log**•i•cal
bac•te•ri•**ol**•o•gist
bac•te•ri•**ol**•o•gy
bad
badge
badg•er
bad•ly
bad•min•ton
bad•mouth

baf•fle
bag
ba•gel
bag•gage
bagged
bag•ging
bag•gy
bag•pip•er
bag•pipes
bail (sounds like "bale")
　She paid his bail.
bail•iff
bail out
bait
bake
bak•er•y
bak•ing
bak•ing **pow**•der
bak•ing **so**•da
bal•ance
bal•anc•ing
bal•co•nies
bal•con•y
bald
bald•ness
bale (sounds like "bail")
　A bale of hay fell
　on him.
Bal•kan
ball (sounds like
　"bawl")
　Throw the ball gently.

bal•lad
bal•last
ball bear•ings
bal•le•ri•na
bal•let
bal•lis•tics
bal•loon
bal•lot
ball•play•er
ball•point
ball•room
balm•i•ness
balm•y
bal•sa
bal•sam
Bal•tic
Bal•ti•more
bam•boo
bam•boo•zle
ban
ba•nan•a
band
band•age
band•ag•ing
ban•dan•na
ban•dit
band•mas•ter
band•wag•on
bang
ban•gle
bangs
ban•ish
ban•ish•ment
ban•is•ter

ban•jo
ban•jos (or
  ban•joes)
bank
bank•er
bank•ing
bank•rupt
bank•rupt•cy
banned
ban•ner
ban•ning
ban•quet
ban•tam
ban•ter
bap•tize
bap•tiz•ing
bar
bar•bar•i•an

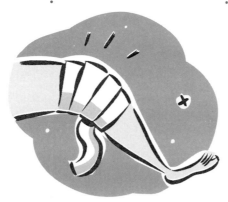

bandage

bar•bar•i•an•ism
bar•bar•ic
bar•be•cue
bar•be•cu•ing

barbed wire
bar•ber
bar•ber•shop
Bar•ce•lo•na
bar code
bare (sounds like
  "bear")
It's too cold to run
around bare.
bare•back
bare•faced
bare•foot
bare•head•ed
bare•ly
bar•gain
barge
barg•ing
bar graph
bar•i•tone
bar•i•um
bark
bar•ley
bar mitz•vah
barn
bar•na•cle
barn•storm•ing
barn•yard
ba•rom•e•ter
bar•o•met•ric
bar•on (sounds like
  "barren")
The baron lives in a
palace.
bar•on•ess

ba•**roque**

bar•racks

bar•ra•**cu**•da

bar•rel

bar•ren (sounds like
   "baron")

*No crops grew on the
barren fields.*

bar•**rette**

bar•ri•cade

bar•ri•cad•ed

bar•ri•er

bar•ri•o

bar•ris•ter

bar•ten•der

bar•ter

base (sounds like
   "bass")

*She slid into third
base.*

base•ball

base•board

base•less

base•ment

bas•es (sounds like
   "basis")

Cover all your bases.

bash

bash•ful

ba•sic

ba•si•cal•ly

ba•sin

ba•sis (sounds like
   "bases")

*This is the basis of
our idea.*

bask

bas•ket

bas•ket•ball

bas mitz•vah

bass (sounds like
   "base")

He has a bass voice.
(rhymes with "class")
We fished for bass.

bass drum

bas•**soon**

baste

bat

batch

bath (n.)

bathe (v.)

bath•ing suit

bath•robe

bath•room

bath•tub

ba•**tik**

bat mitz•vah

ba•**ton**

bat•**tal**•ion

bat•ter

bat•ter•ing **ram**

bat•ter•y

bat•tle

bat•tle•field

bat•tle•ground

bat•tle•ship

bau•ble

bawd•y

bawl (sounds like
   "ball")

He'll bawl like a baby.

bay

bay•o•net

bay•ou

ba•**zaar** (sounds like
   "bizarre")

*I bought this at the
bazaar.*

be

beach (sounds like
   "beech")

This beach is rocky.

bea•con

bead

bea•gle

beak

beak•er

beam

bean

bean•stalk

bear (sounds like
   "bare")

*The grizzly bear
growled loudly.*

beard

bear•ing

bear•skin

beast

beat (sounds like
   "beet")

*He likes to beat
his drum.*

beau•**ti**•cian
beau•ti•ful
beau•ty
bea•ver
be•**cause**
beck•on
be•**come**
be•**com**•ing
bed
be•**daz**•zle
be•**daz**•zling
bed•bug
bed•clothes
bed•ding
bed•fel•low
bed•lam
bed•ou•in
be•**drag**•gle
be•**drag**•gled
bed•rid•den
bed•rock
bed•room
bed•side
bed•spread
bed•time
bee
beech (sounds like "beach")
She climbed the beech tree.
beef
beef•steak
bee•hive
bee•line

been
beep
beer (sounds like "bier")
We don't serve beer to minors.
beet (sounds like "beat")
He makes delicious beet soup.
Bee•tho•ven
bee•tle
be•**fit**•ting
be•**fore**
be•**fore**•hand
be•**friend**
beg
be•**gan**
beg•gar
beg•ging
be•**gin**
be•**gin**•ner
be•**gin**•ning
be•**go**•ni•a
be•**grudge**
be•**guile**
be•**guil**•ing
be•**half**
be•**have**
be•**hav**•ior
be•**head**
be•**held**
be•**he**•moth
be•**hind**

be•**hold**
be•**hoove**
beige
be•ing
Bei•rut
be•**la**•bor
be•**lat**•ed
belch
bel•fry
Bel•gian (adj.)
Bel•gium (n.)
be•**lief**
be•**liev**•a•ble
be•**lieve**
be•**liev**•ing
be•**lit**•tle
be•**lit**•tling
bell
bell•boy
bell•hop
bel•li•cose
bel•lies
bel•**lig**•er•ence
bel•**lig**•er•ent
bel•low
bel•lows
bel•ly
bel•ly **but**•ton
be•**long**
be•**lov**•ed
be•**low**
belt
bench
bend

be•neath
ben•e•fac•tor
ben•e•fi•cial
ben•e•fit
ben•e•fit•ed
ben•e•fit•ing
be•nev•o•lence
be•nev•o•lent
be•nign
be•queath
be•rate
be•rat•ing
be•reaved
be•reave•ment
be•ret
ber•ries
ber•ry (sounds like "bury")
What kind of berry grows on this tree?
ber•serk
berth (sounds like "birth")
He slept in the upper berth on the train.
be•seech
be•side
be•sides
be•siege
best
be•stow
bet
Beth•le•hem
be•tray

be•tray•al
be•tray•er
bet•ter
bet•ting
be•tween
bev•er•age
be•ware
be•wil•der
be•wil•der•ment
be•witch
be•yond
bi•as
bi•ased
bi•ath•lon
Bi•ble
bib•li•cal
bib•li•og•ra•phy
bi•cam•er•al
bi•car•bo•nate
bi•cen•ten•ni•al
bi•ceps

bick•er
bi•coast•al
bi•cus•pid
bi•cy•cle
bi•cy•clist
bid
bid•der
bid•ding
bide
bier (sounds like "beer")
The corpse was placed on the funeral bier.
bi•fo•cals
big
big•ger
big•horn
big•ot
big•ot•ed
big•ot•ry
bike
bi•ki•ni
bile
bi•lin•gual
bill
bill•board
bill•fold
bil•liards
bil•lion
bil•lion•aire
bil•low
bil•low•y
bin
bi•na•ry

(biceps)

bind
bind·er
binge
bin·go
bin·**oc**·u·lars
bi·o·de·**grad**·a·ble
bi·o·di·**ver**·si·ty
bi·**og**·ra·pher
bi·o·**graph**·i·cal
bi·**og**·ra·phy
bi·**ol**·o·gy
bi·**on**·ic
bi·o·rhythm
bi·plane
birch
bird
birth (sounds like "berth")

We all celebrated the birth of the baby.

birth·day
birth·mark
birth·place
birth·rate
birth·right
birth·stone
bis·cuit
bi·sect
bi·**sec**·tion
bish·op
bi·son
bit
bite (sounds like "byte")

He took a big bite of cake.

bit·ing
bit·ter
bi·**zarre** (sounds like "bazaar")

Her outfit is bizarre.

blab
blabbed
blab·ber
blab·bing
blab·ber·mouth

(blabbermouth)

black
black·ball
black·ber·ry
black·bird
black·board
black·en
black eye
Black·foot
black hole
black·jack

black·mail
black·out
black·smith
black·top
blad·der
blade
blame
blame·less
bland
blank
blan·ket
blare
blar·ing
blas·phe·my
blast
blast·off
bla·tant
blaze
blaz·er
blaz·ing
bleach
bleach·ers
bleak
blear·y
bleed
blem·ish
blend
blend·er
bless
bless·ed
blew (sounds like "blue")

The bugler blew the horn.

blight

blimp

blind

blind•er

blind•fold

blind•ness

blink

bliss

bliss•ful

blis•ter

bliz•zard

bloat

bloat•ed

blob

bloc (sounds like "block")

The bloc of nations voted for peace.

block (sounds like "bloc")

Here's a block of wood to play with.

block•**ade**

block•**ad**•ing

blond

blood

blood•hound

blood•shed

blood•shot

blood•stream

blood•thirst•y

blood **ves**•sel

blood•y

bloom

bloom•ers

blos•som

blot

blotch

blotch•y

blot•ter

blot•ting

blouse

blow

blow•er

blow•torch

blow•up

blub•ber

bludg•eon

blue (sounds like "blew")

I wore my blue shirt.

Blue•beard

blue•ber•ry

blue•ber•ries

blue•bird

blue•fish

blue•grass

blue jay

blue jeans

blue•print

blues

blue whale

bluff

blun•der

blunt

blur

blurb

blurred

blur•ring

blur•ry

blurt

blush

blus•ter

blus•ter•y

bo•a con•**stric**•tor

boar (sounds like "bore")

The wild boar ran into the woods.

board

board•er

board•ing

boast

boast•ful

boat

boat•house

boat•ing

bob

bobbed

bob•bin

bob•bing

bob•by **pin**

bob•cat

bob•sled

bob•tail

bob•white

bode

bod•ing

bod•y

bod•y•guard

bog

bogged

bog•gy
bo•gus
boil
boil•er
boil•ing **point**
bois•ter•ous
bold
bold•face
boll wee•vil
bol•ster
bolt
bomb
bom•**bard**
bom•**bard**•ment
bom•**bas**•tic
Bom•**bay**
bomb•er
bomb•proof
bomb•shell
bo•na fide
bo•**nan**•za
Bo•na•parte
bon•bon
bond
bond•age
bone
bone-dry
bon•fire
bon•go **drum**
bon•net
bon•sai
  also pronounced
  bon•**sai**
bo•nus

bon voy•**age**
bon•y
boo•by **trap**
boog•ie-**woog**•ie
book
book•case
book club
book•end
book•keep•er
book•keep•ing
book•let
book•mark
book•mo•bile
book•store
book•worm
boom
boo•mer•ang
boon
boost
boos•ter
boot
booth
boot•leg
boo•ty
booze
bor•der
bore (sounds like
  "boar")
*I hope my story
didn't bore you.*
bore•dom
bor•ing
born (sounds like
  "borne")

*My brother was born
on a Tuesday.*
borne (sounds like
  "born")
*The donkey has borne
a heavy load.*
bor•ough (sounds like
  "burro" and "burrow")
*He lives in another
borough of the city.*
bor•row
bos•om
boss
boss•y
Bos•ton
bo•**tan**•i•cal
bot•a•nist
bot•a•ny
both
both•er
both•er•some
bot•tle
bot•tle•neck
bot•tling
bot•tom
bough (rhymes with
  "wow")
*She climbed out onto
the bough of the tree.*
bought
bouil•lon (sounds like
  "bullion")
*Drink this clear
chicken bouillon.*
boul•der

bou•le•vard
bounce
bounc•ing
bound
bound•a•ries
bound•a•ry
bound•less
boun•ti•ful
boun•ty
bou•**quet**
bour•bon
bout
bou•**tique**
bo•vine
bow (rhymes with "go")

She tied a bow in her hair.

bow (rhymes with "cow")

Take a bow after your performance.

bow•els
bowl
bow•leg•ged
bowl•ing
box
box•car
box•er
box•es
boy
boy•cott
boy•friend
boy•hood

bra
brace
brace•let
brac•ing
brack•et
brag
bragged
Brah•ma
braid

braid

Braille
brain
brain•child
brain•storm
brain•wash
brain•y
brake (sounds like "break")

Step on the brake to stop the car.

brake•man
brak•ing
bram•ble
bran
branch

branch•es
brand
bran•dish
brand-new
brand•y
brass
brass•y
brat
bra•**va**•do
brave
brav•er•y
bra•vo
brawl
brawn•i•er
bra•zen
Bra•**zil**
breach
bread
breadth
bread•win•ner
break (sounds like "brake")

I didn't break it.

break•down
break•er
break•fast
break-in
break•neck
break•through
break•wa•ter
breast
breast•bone
breast•plate
breast•stroke

breath (n.)
breathe (v.)
breath·er
breath·ing
breath·less
breath·tak·ing
breech·es
breed
breeze
breez·i·ly
breez·y
brev·i·ty
brew
brew·er·y
bri·ar
bribe
brib·ing
brick
brick·lay·er
brick·work
brid·al (sounds like "bridle")

The bridal party has two bridesmaids.

bride
bride·groom
brides·maid
bridge
bri·dle (sounds like "bridal")

Ride the horse on the bridle path.

brief
brief·case

bri·er
brig
bri·gade
bright
bright·en
bril·liance
bril·liant
brim
brim·ful

bricklayer

brim·med
brim·ming
brine
bring
brink
brisk
bris·tle
bris·tling
Brit·ain

Brit·ish
brit·tle
broach (sounds like "brooch")

He hated to broach the subject.

broad
broad·cast
broad·en
broad-mind·ed
broad·side
bro·cade
broc·co·li
bro·chure
broil·er
broke
bro·ken
bro·ken·heart·ed
bro·ker
bro·ker·age
bron·chi·al
bron·chi·tis
bron·co
bron·to·saur·us
bronze
Bronze Age
brooch (sounds like "broach")

She wore a diamond brooch.

brood
brook
Brook·lyn
broom

broom·stick
broth
broth·er
broth·er·hood
broth·er-in-law
broth·ers-in-law
brought
brow
brow·beat
brown
brown·ie
brown·out
brown·stone
browse
brows·ing
bruise
bruis·ing
brunch
bru·**nette**
brunt
brush
brusque
Brus·sels sprout
bru·tal
bru·**tal**·i·ty
brute
bub·ble
bub·bling
bub·bly
bu·**bon**·ic
buc·ca·**neer**
buck
buck·a·roo
buck·board

buck·et
buck·le
buck·ling
buck·shot
buck·skin
buck·tooth
buck·wheat
bud
Bud·dha
Bud·dhism
Bud·dhist
bud·ding
bud·dy
budge
budg·et
budg·ing
Bue·nos **Ai**·res
buff
buf·fa·lo
buff·er
buf·fet
buf·**foon**
bug
bugged
bug·ging
bug·gy
bu·gle
bu·gler
build
build·ing
built
built-in
bulb
bulge

bulg·ing
bulk
bulk·i·er
bulk·i·est
bulk·y
bull
bull·dog
bull·doz·er
bul·let
bul·le·tin
bul·let·proof
bull·fight
bull·frog
bul·lion (sounds like
  "bouillon")
  There is gold bullion
  in the bank.
bull's-eye
bul·ly
bum·ble·bee
bum·bling
bump
bump·er
bump·i·er
bump·i·est
bump·y
bun
bunch
bun·dle
bun·dling
bun·ga·low
bun·gee cord
bun·gle
bunk

bun·ker
bunk·house
bun·ny
Bun·sen **burn·**er
bunt
bunt·ing
buoy
buoy·ant
bur (*or* **burr**)
bur·den
bur·den·some
bu·reau
bu·**reauc·**ra·cy
bu·reau·**crat·**ic
bur·ger
bur·glar
bur·glar·ize
bur·glar·proof
bur·glar·y
bur·i·al
bur·ied
bur·ies
bur·lap
bur·**lesque**
bur·li·ness
bur·ly
Bur·ma
Bur·**mese**
burn
burn·er
bur·nish
burnt
burp

bur·ri·to
bur·ro (sounds like
    "borough" and
    "burrow")
*She rode a little burro
into town.*
bur·row (sounds like
    "borough" and
    "burro")
*The rabbit tried to
burrow in the yard.*
burst
bur·y (sounds like
    "berry")
*Let's bury the
treasure.*
bur·y·ing
bus
bush
bush·el
bush·man
bush·whack
bush·y
bus·i·er
bus·i·est
busi·ness
busi·ness·like
bust
bus·tle
bus·tling
bus·y
bus·y·bod·y
but
butch·er

but·ler
but·ter
but·ter·cup
but·ter·fin·gers
but·ter·flies
but·ter·fly
but·ter·milk
but·ter·scotch
but·ter·y
but·ton
but·ton·hole
but·tress
buy (sounds like
    "by")
*How many pears did
you buy?*
buzz
buz·zard
buzz·er
by (sounds like "buy")
*This book is by
Mark Twain.*
by·gone
by·law
by·pass
by·prod·uct
by·stand·er
byte (sounds like
    "bite")
*A byte is a unit of
computer memory.*
by·word
Byz·an·tine

cab

cab•bage

cab•in

cab•i•net

ca•ble

ca•boose

ca•ca•o

cack•le

ca•coph•o•ny

cac•tus

ca•det

Cae•sar

ca•fé

caf•e•te•ri•a

caf•feine

  also pronounced

  caf•feine

caf•tan

cage

ca•gey

Cai•ro

ca•jole

Ca•jun

cake

ca•lam•i•ty

cal•ci•um

cal•cu•late

cal•cu•lat•ing

cal•cu•la•tor

cal•en•dar

calf

cal•i•co

Cal•i•for•nia

call

cal•lig•ra•pher

cal•lig•ra•phy

call•ing

cal•lous

cal•low

calm

cal•o•rie

calves

ca•lyp•so

cam•cord•er

came

cam•el

Cam•e•lot

cam•e•o

camera

cam•er•a

cam•er•a•per•son

cam•ou•flage

camp

cam•paign

cam•per

camp•fire

cam•phor

camp•us

can

Can•a•da

Ca•na•di•an

ca•nal

ca•nar•y

can•cel

can•celed

can•cel•ing

can•cel•la•tion

can•cer

can•cer•ous

can•de•la•bra

can•did

can•di•da•cy

can•di•date

can•died

can•dle

can•dle•light

can•dy

cane

ca•nine

canned

can•ner•y

can•ni•bal

can•non (sounds like "canon")

  The rebels fired the cannon.

can•ny

ca•**noe**

ca•**noe**•ing

can•on (sounds like "cannon")

The priest knew church canon.

can•o•py

can't

can•ta•loupe

can•**tan**•ker•ous

can•**ta**•ta

can•**teen**

can•ter (sounds like "cantor")

This horse loves to canter.

Can•ton•**ese**

can•tor (sounds like "canter")

The cantor sings in the synagogue.

can•vas (sounds like "canvass")

The tent is made of canvas.

can•vass (sounds like "canvas")

Canvass the people for their votes.

can•yon

cap

ca•pa•**bil**•i•ties

ca•pa•**bil**•i•ty

ca•pa•ble

ca•**pac**•i•ty

cape

ca•per

cap•ful

cap•il•lar•y

cap•i•tal (sounds like "capitol")

Begin each sentence with a capital letter.

cap•i•tal•ism

cap•i•tal•ist

cap•i•tol (sounds like "capital")

The legislature meets in the capitol building.

cap•puc•**ci**•no

ca•**pri**•cious

capsize

cap•size

cap•**siz**•ing

cap•sule

cap•tain

cap•tion

cap•ti•vate

cap•ti•vat•ing

cap•tive

cap•**tiv**•i•ty

cap•tor

cap•ture

cap•tur•ing

car

car•a•mel

car•at (sounds like "karat," "caret," and "carrot")

This ring has a one-carat diamond.

car•a•van

car•bide

car•bine

car•bo•**hy**•drates

car•bon

car•bu•re•tor

car•cass

card

card•board

car•di•ac

car•di•gan

car•di•nal

care

ca•**reer**

care•free

care•ful

care•giv•er

care•less

car•**ess**

car•et (sounds like

"carat," "carrot," and "karat")

The caret shows where to insert the word.

care•tak•er

car•fare

car•go

Ca•**rib**•be•an

car•i•bou

car•i•ca•ture

car•i•ca•tur•ist

car•jack

car•**load**

car•**na**•tion

car•ni•val

car•ni•vore

car•**niv**•o•rous

car•ob

car•ol

car•ol•er

Car•o•**li**•na

ca•**rouse**

ca•**rous**•ing

carp

car•pen•ter

car•pet

car•pet•bag•ger

car•pet•ing

car•pool (v.)

car pool (n.)

car•riage

car•ried

car•ri•er

car•ries

car•rot (sounds like "carat," "caret," and "karat")

Did you slice a carrot into the salad?

car•ry

car•ry•ing

car•sick

cart

carte blanche

car•ti•lage

car•**tog**•ra•pher

car•**tog**•ra•phy

car•ton

car•**toon**

car•**toon**•ist

car•tridge

cart•wheel

carve

carv•ing

cas•**cade**

cas•**cad**•ing

case

case•ment

cash

cash•ew

ca•**shier**

cash•mere

ca•**si**•no

cask

cas•ket

cas•se•role

cas•**sette**

cast (sounds like "caste")

She had a cast on her broken leg.

cast•a•way

caste (sounds like "cast")

She belongs to a high caste in that society.

cast iron

cas•tle

cas•u•al

cas•u•al•ty

cat

cat•a•comb

cat•a•log (*or* cat•a•logue)

cat•a•lyst

cat•a•ma•**ran**

cat•a•pult

cat•a•ract

ca•**tas**•tro•phe

ca•ta•**stroph**•ic

cat•bird

catch

catch•er

catch•y

cat•e•**gor**•i•cal

cat•e•go•rize

cat•e•go•ry

ca•ter

ca•ter•er

cat•er•pil•lar

cat•fish

ca•**thar**•sis
ca•**the**•dral
cath•ode-ray
Cath•o•lic
Ca•**thol**•i•cism
cat•nap
cat•nip
cat-o'-**nine**-tails
CAT scan
cat•sup
cat•tail
cat•tle
cat•ty
Cau•**ca**•sian
cau•cus
caught
caul•dron
cau•li•flow•er
caulk
cause
cause•way
caus•tic
cau•tion
cau•tion•ar•y
cau•tious
cav•al•**cade**
cav•a•**lier**
cav•al•ry
cave
cave-in
cave•man
cav•ern
cav•ern•ous
cave•wom•an

cav•i•ar
cav•i•ties
cav•i•ty
cease
cease-fire
cease•less
ceas•ing
ce•dar
ceil•ing
cel•e•brate
cel•e•brat•ing
cel•e•**bra**•tion
ce•**leb**•ri•ties
ce•**leb**•ri•ty
cel•er•y
ce•**les**•tial
cell (sounds like "sell")
The prisoner slept in his cell.
cel•lar
cel•list
cel•lo
cel•los
cel•lu•lar
cel•lu•loid
cel•lu•lose
Cel•si•us
Celt•ic
ce•**ment**
cem•e•ter•y
cen•sor
cen•sor•ship
cen•sure
cen•sur•ing

cen•sus
cent (sounds like "scent" and "sent")
A cent isn't worth much today.
cen•taur
cen•**ten**•ni•al
cen•ter
cen•ter•piece
cen•ti•grade
cen•ti•me•ter
cen•ti•pede
cen•tral
cen•**tri**•fu•gal
cen•**trip**•e•tal
cen•tu•ries
cen•**tu**•ri•on
cen•tu•ry
ce•**ram**•ic
ce•**ram**•ics
ce•re•al (sounds like "serial")
I eat two bowls of cereal every morning.
cer•e•**bel**•lum
ce•**re**•bral
cer•e•**mo**•ni•al
cer•e•**mo**•nies
cer•e•**mo**•ni•ous
cer•e•**mo**•ny
cer•tain
cer•tain•ty
cer•**tif**•i•cate
cer•ti•fi•**ca**•tion

cer•ti•fied
cer•ti•fies
cer•ti•fy
cer•ti•fy•ing
chafe
chaf•ing
cha•grin
chain
chair
chair•lift
chair•man
chair•per•son
chair•wom•an
cha•let
chal•ice
chalk
chalk•board
chalk•y
chal•lenge
cham•ber
cha•me•le•on
cham•ois
cham•pagne
cham•pi•on
cham•pi•on•ship
chance
chan•cel•lor
chanc•ing
chan•de•lier
change
change•a•bil•i•ty
change•a•ble
chan•nel
chant

Cha•nu•kah (or
  Ha•nuk•kah)
cha•os
cha•ot•ic
chap
chap•el
chap•lain
chaps

(chaps)

chap•ter
char•ac•ter
char•ac•ter•is•tic
char•ac•ter•i•za•tion
char•ac•ter•ize
cha•rade
char•coal
charge
charg•ing
char•i•ot
char•i•ot•eer
cha•ris•ma

char•i•ta•ble
char•i•ties
char•i•ty
charm
charm•ing
chart
char•ter
chase
chas•ing
chasm
chas•sis
chas•tise
  also pronounced
  chas•tise
chat
châ•teau
chat•ted
chat•ter
chat•ting
chat•ty
chauf•feur
  also pronounced
  chauf•feur
chau•vin•ist
cheap
cheap•en
cheat
cheat•ed
cheat•ing
check
check•book
check•er•board
check•ers
check•out

check•room
check•up
cheek
cheek•y
cheer
cheer•ful
cheer•ful•ly
cheer•i•ly
cheer•lead•er
cheer•less
cheer•y
cheese
chees•y
chee•tah
chef
chem•i•cal
chem•ist
chem•is•try
che•mo•**ther**•a•py
che•**nille**
cher•ish
Cher•o•kee
cher•ry
cher•ub
chess
chess•board
chest
chest•nut
chew
chew•ing
chew•ing **gum**
chew•y
Chey•**enne**
Chi•**ca**•go

Chi•**ca**•na
Chi•**ca**•no
chick
chick•a•dee
chick•en
chick•en **pox**
chick•pea
chic•o•ry
chide
chid•ing
chief
chiefs
chief•tain
chif•**fon**
chig•ger

(**Chihuahua**)

Chi•**hua**•hua
child
child•bear•ing
child•birth
child•hood
child•ish

chil•dren
Chi•le
chil•i (sounds like "chilly")
This chili has two kinds of beans.
chill
chill•i•ness
chill•y (sounds like "chili")
Take a sweater; it's chilly.
chime
chim•ing
chim•ney
chim•pan•**zee**
  also pronounced chim•**pan**•zee
chin
chi•na
Chi•na
Chi•na•town
chin•**chil**•la
Chi•**nese**
chink
chinned
chin•ning
Chi•**nook**
chip
chip•munk
chipped
Chip•pe•wa
chip•ping
chi•ro•prac•tor
chirp

chis•el
chis•el•er
chiv•al•rous
chiv•al•ry
chlo•rine
chlo•ro•**fluor**•o•car•bon
chlo•ro•form
chlo•ro•phyll
choc•o•late
Choc•taw
choice
choic•est
choir
choke
chok•ing
chol•e•ra
cho•**les**•ter•ol
choose
choos•ing
chop
chopped
chop•per
chop•ping
chop•py
chop•sticks
cho•ral
chord (sounds like "cord")

Play this chord on the piano.

chore
cho•re•**og**•ra•pher
cho•re•**og**•ra•phy

chor•tle
chort•ling
cho•rus
chose
cho•sen
chow•der
Christ
chris•ten•ing
Chris•tian
Chris•ti•**an**•i•ty
Christ•mas
chro•mo•some
chron•ic
chron•i•cal•ly
chron•i•cle
chron•i•cling
chron•o•**log**•i•cal
chrys•a•lis
chry•**san**•the•mum
chub•bi•er
chub•bi•est
chub•by
chuck
chuck•le
chuck•ling
chuck wag•on
chug
chum
chum•mi•ly
chum•my
chunk
chunk•y
church
church•go•er

church•yard
churl•ish
churn
chute (sounds like "shoot")

Throw the laundry down the chute.

chut•ney
ci•der
ci•**gar**
cig•a•**rette** (*or* cig•a•**ret**)
cin•der
cin•e•ma
cin•na•mon
cir•ca
cir•cle
cir•cling
cir•cuit
cir•cu•lar
cir•cu•late
cir•cu•lat•ing
cir•cu•la•tion
cir•cu•la•to•ry
cir•**cum**•fer•ence
cir•cum•spect
cir•cum•stance
cir•cus
ci•**ta**•tion
cite (sounds like "sight" and "site")

Can you cite Shakespeare on the subject of love?

cit•ies

cit•i•zen
cit•i•zen•ship
cit•rus
cit•y
civ•ic
civ•ics
civ•il
ci•**vil**•ian
civ•i•li•**za**•tion
civ•i•lize
civ•i•**liz**•ing
clad
claim
clam
clam•bake
clam•mi•ness
clam•my
clam•or
clamp
clan
clap
clap•board
clapped
clap•ping
clap•trap
clar•i•fi•**ca**•tion
clar•i•fied
clar•i•fies
clar•i•fy
clar•i•**net**
clar•i•ty
clash
clasp
class

clas•sic
clas•si•cal
clas•si•fied
clas•si•fies
clas•si•fy
class•mate
class•room
clas•sy
clat•ter
clause (sounds like
   "claws")
   This sentence has a
   dependent clause.
claus•tro•**pho**•bi•a
claw
claws (sounds like
   "clause")
   The cat dug its claws
   into the curtains.
clay
clean
clean•li•ness
cleanse
cleans•er
clear
clear•ance
clear•ing
clef
cleft
clem•en•cy
clem•ent
clench
Cle•o•**pat**•ra
cler•gy

cler•i•cal
clerk
clev•er
cli•**ché**
click
cli•ent
cli•en•**tele**
cliff
cliff-han•ger
cli•mate
cli•max
climb
clinch
clinch•er
cling
clin•ic
clin•i•cal
cli•**ni**•cian
clip
clip art
clip•board
clipped
clip•per
clip•ping
clique
cloak
cloak•room
clob•ber
clock
clock•wise
clock•work
clod
clog
clois•ter

clone

close

closed-cir•cuit

clos•et

close-up

clot

cloth (n.)

clothe (v.)

clothes

clothes•line

cloth•ing

cloud

cloud•burst

cloud•i•ness

cloud•y

clove

clo•ver

clown

clown•ish

cloy•ing

club

clue

clump

clum•si•ly

clum•si•ness

clum•sy

clus•ter

clutch

clut•ter

coach

coach•man

co•ag•u•late

co•ag•u•lat•ing

coal

co•a•li•tion

coarse (sounds like "course")

This material is coarse and scratchy.

coast

coast guard

coast•line

coat

coat•ing

coat of arms

coat•room

coax

co•balt

cob•bler

cob•ble•stone

co•bra

cob•web

co•caine

cock

cock•a•too

cock•er span•iel

cock•pit

cock•roach

cock•y

co•coa

co•co•nut

co•coon

cod•dle

cod•dling

code

co•ed•u•ca•tion

co•erce

co•erc•ing

co•er•cion

co•er•cive

cof•fee

cof•fin

cog

co•her•ent

coil

coin

co•in•cide

co•in•ci•dence

co•in•ci•den•tal

col•an•der

cold

cold•er

cold•est

cold-blood•ed

cole•slaw

col•i•se•um

col•lab•o•rate

col•lab•o•rat•ing

col•lab•o•ra•tion

cockatoo

col•**lage**
col•**lapse**
col•**laps**•i•ble
col•**laps**•ing
col•lar
col•lards
col•league
col•**lect**
col•**lec**•tion
col•lege
col•**lide**
col•**lid**•ing
col•lie
col•**li**•sion
col•**lo**•qui•al
col•**lo**•qui•al•ism
co•**logne**
co•lon
colo•nel
co•**lo**•ni•al
col•o•nies
col•on•ist
col•o•nize
col•o•ny
col•or
Col•o•**ra**•do
col•or•ful
col•or•ing
col•or•ize
col•or•less
co•**los**•sal
colt
col•um•bine
Co•**lum**•bus **Day**

col•umn
col•um•nist
co•ma
comb
com•bat
com•bi•**na**•tion
com•**bine**
com•**bin**•ing
com•**bus**•ti•ble
com•**bus**•tion
come
co•**me**•di•an

comedian

com•e•dies
com•e•dy
com•et
com•fort
com•fort•a•ble
com•ic
com•i•cal

com•ic **book**
com•ic **strip**
com•ma
com•**mand**
com•**mand**•er
com•**mand**•ment
com•**man**•do
com•**mem**•o•rate
com•**mem**•o•rat•ing
com•mem•o•**ra**•tion
com•**mence**
com•**mence**•ment
com•**menc**•ing
com•**mend**
com•**mend**•a•ble
com•men•**da**•tion
com•ment
com•men•tar•y
com•men•ta•tor
com•merce
com•**mer**•cial
com•**mer**•cial•ize
com•**mis**•er•ate
com•**mis**•er•at•ing
com•mis•er•**a**•tion
com•**mis**•sion
com•**mit**
com•**mit**•ment
com•**mit**•ted
com•**mit**•tee
com•**mod**•i•ty
com•mon
com•mon
de•**nom**•i•na•tor

com•mon•ly
Com•mon Mar•ket
com•mon•place
com•mon sense
com•mon•wealth
com•mo•tion
com•mu•nal
com•mune (n.)
com•mune (v.)
com•mu•ni•ca•ble
com•mu•ni•cate
com•mu•ni•cat•ing
com•mu•ni•ca•tion
Com•mun•ion
com•mu•ni•qué
com•mun•ism
Com•mun•ist Par•ty
com•mu•ni•ties
com•mu•ni•ty
com•mut•er
com•pact (n.)
com•pact (v.)
com•pa•nies
com•pan•ion
com•pa•ny
com•pa•ra•ble
com•par•a•tive
com•pare
com•par•ing
com•par•i•son
com•part•ment
com•pass
com•pas•sion
com•pas•sion•ate

com•pat•i•ble
com•pel
com•pelled
com•pel•ling
com•pen•sate
com•pen•sat•ing
com•pen•sa•tion
com•pete
com•pe•tent
com•pet•ing
com•pe•ti•tion
com•pet•i•tive
com•pet•i•tor
com•pile
com•pla•cent
com•plain
com•plaint
com•ple•ment (sounds
  like "compliment")
*Ice cream will
complement the pie.*
com•plete
com•plet•ing
com•ple•tion
com•plex (adj.)
com•plex (n.)
com•plex•ion
com•plex•i•ty
com•pli•cate
com•pli•cat•ed
com•pli•cat•ing
comp•li•ca•tion
com•plied
com•plies

com•pli•ment (sounds
  like "complement")
*Thanks for the
flattering compliment.*
com•pli•men•ta•ry
com•ply
com•po•nent
com•pose
com•pos•ing
com•pos•ite
com•po•si•tion
com•post
com•po•sure
com•pound (adj. and n.)
com•pound (v.)
com•pre•hend
com•pre•hen•sion
com•pre•hen•sive
com•press (v.)
com•press (n.)
com•prise
com•pris•ing
com•pro•mise
com•pro•mis•ing
com•pul•so•ry
com•pu•ta•tion
com•pute
com•put•er
com•put•ing
com•rade
con•cave
con•ceal
con•cede
con•ced•ing

con•**ceit**
con•**ceit**•ed
con•**ceive**
con•**ceiv**•ing
con•cen•trate
con•cen•trat•ing
con•cen•**tra**•tion
con•**cen**•tric
con•cept
con•**cern**
con•**cerned**
con•**cern**•ing
con•cert
con•**cer**•to
con•**ces**•sion
conch
con•**cise**
con•**clude**
con•**clud**•ing
con•**clu**•sion
con•**coct**
con•cord
con•crete
con•**cur**
con•**curred**
con•**cus**•sion
con•**demn**
con•dem•**na**•tion
con•den•**sa**•tion
con•**dense**
con•**dens**•ing
con•de•**scend**•ing
con•**di**•tion
con•**di**•tion•al

con•**di**•tion•er
con•**do**•lence
con•do•**min**•i•um
con•dor
con•duct (n.)

(**conch**)

con•**duct** (v.)
con•**duc**•ting
con•**duc**•tor
cone
con•**fed**•er•a•cies
con•**fed**•er•a•cy
con•**fed**•er•ate
con•fed•er•**a**•tion
con•**fer**
con•fer•ence
con•**ferred**
con•**fer**•ring
con•**fess**
con•**fet**•ti
con•**fide**
con•fi•dence
con•fi•dent

con•fi•**den**•tial
con•**fid**•ing
con•**fine**
con•**fin**•ing
con•**firm**
con•fir•**ma**•tion
con•fis•cate
con•fis•cat•ing
con•fla•**gra**•tion
con•flict (n.)
con•**flict** (v.)
con•flu•ence
con•**form**
con•**form**•ing
con•**form**•ist
con•**front**
con•fron•**ta**•tion
Con•**fu**•cian•ism
Con•**fu**•cius
con•**fuse**
con•**fus**•ing
con•**fu**•sion
con•**ge**•ni•al
con•ge•ni•**al**•i•ty
con•**ges**•ted
con•**ges**•tion
con•**glom**•er•ate
con•**glom**•er•**a**•tion
con•**grat**•u•late
con•**grat**•u•lat•ing
con•grat•u•**la**•tions
con•gre•gate
con•gre•gat•ing
con•gre•**ga**•tion

Con•gress
con•**gres**•sio•nal
con•**gru**•ent
con•i•fer
con•ju•gate
con•ju•gat•ing
con•ju•**ga**•tion
con•**junc**•tion
con•jure
con•jur•er (*or*
  con•jur•or)
con•jur•ing
con•**nect**
Con•**nect**•i•cut
con•**nec**•tion
con•**nec**•tive
con•**nive**
con•**niv**•ing
con•nois•**seur**
con•quer
con•quest
con•science
con•sci•**en**•tious
con•scious
con•**sec**•u•tive
con•**sen**•sus
con•**sent**
con•se•quence
con•ser•**va**•tion
con•**serv**•a•tive
con•**serv**•a•to•ry
con•**serve**
con•**serv**•ing
con•**sid**•er

con•**sid**•er•a•ble
con•**sid**•er•ate
con•sid•er•**a**•tion
con•**sign**•ment
con•**sist**
con•**sis**•tent
con•**sole** (v.)
con•sole (n.)
con•**sol**•i•date
con•**sol**•i•dat•ing
con•sol•i•**da**•tion
con•**sol**•ing
con•so•nant
con•**spic**•u•ous
con•**spir**•a•cies
con•**spir**•a•cy
con•**spire**
con•**spir**•ing
con•sta•ble
con•stant
Con•stan•ti•**no**•ple
con•stel•**la**•tion
con•ster•**na**•tion
con•sti•pat•ed
con•sti•**pa**•tion
con•**stit**•u•ent
con•**stit**•u•en•cies
con•**stit**•u•en•cy
con•sti•tute
con•sti•tut•ing
con•sti•**tu**•tion
con•sti•**tu**•tion•al
con•**straint**
con•**strict**

con•**stric**•tion
con•**struct**
con•**struc**•tion
con•**struc**•tive
con•sul
con•sul•ar
con•sul•ate
con•**sult**
con•**sul**•tant
con•sul•**ta**•tion
con•**sume**
con•**sum**•er
con•**sum**•ing
con•**sump**•tion
con•tact
con•tact lens
con•**ta**•gious
con•**tain**
con•**tain**•er
con•**tam**•i•nate
con•**tam**•i•nat•ing
con•tam•i•**na**•tion
con•tem•plate
con•tem•plat•ing
con•tem•**pla**•tion
con•**tem**•po•rar•y
con•**tempt**
con•**tempt**•i•ble
con•**tend**
con•tent (n.)
con•**tent** (v. and adj.)
con•**tent**•ed
con•**tent**•ment
con•tents

con•test (n.)
con•**test** (v.)
con•**tes**•tant
con•text
con•ti•nent
con•ti•**nen**•tal
con•**tin**•u•al
con•**tin**•ue
con•**tin**•u•ing
con•ti•**nu**•i•ty
con•**tin**•u•ous
con•**tort**
con•**tor**•tion
con•tract (n.)
con•**tract** (v.)
con•**trac**•tion
con•tra•**dict**
con•tra•**dic**•tion
con•tra•**dic**•to•ry
con•**trap**•tion
con•trar•i•ness
con•trar•y
con•trast (n.)
con•**trast** (v.)
con•**tri**•bute
con•**tri**•but•ing
con•tri•**bu**•tion
con•**trite**
con•**triv**•ance
con•**trive**
con•**triv**•ing
con•**trol**
con•**trolled**
con•**trol**•ling

con•tro•**ver**•sial
con•tro•ver•sies
con•tro•ver•sy
con•va•**lesce**
con•va•**les**•cence
con•va•**les**•cent
con•va•**lesc**•ing
con•**vec**•tion
con•**vene**
con•**ven**•ience
con•**ven**•ient
con•vent
con•**ven**•tion
con•**ven**•tion•al
con•**ven**•tion•**al**•i•ty
con•**verge**
con•**ver**•gence
con•**verg**•ing
con•ver•**sa**•tion
con•ver•**sa**•tion•al
con•**verse**
con•**vers**•ing
con•**ver**•sion
con•**vert**
con•**vert**•i•ble
con•vex
  also pronounced
  con•**vex**
con•**vey**
con•**vey**•ance
con•**vey**•or belt
con•**vict** (v.)
con•vict (n.)
con•**vic**•tion

con•**vince**
con•**vinc**•ing
con•**viv**•i•al
con•vo•**ca**•tion
con•**vok**•ing
con•voy
con•**vulse**
con•**vul**•sion
coo
coo•ing
cook
cook•book
cook•ie
cool
cool•er
cool•ly
coop
co-op
co•**op**•er•ate

convict

co•**op**•er•at•ing
co•op•er•**a**•tion
co•op•er•a•tive
co•**or**•di•nate
co•**or**•di•nat•ed
co•**or**•di•nat•ing
co•**or**•di•**na**•tion
co•**or**•di•na•tor
cope
Co•pen•**ha**•gen
Co•**per**•ni•cus
cop•ied
cop•ies
co•pi•lot
cop•ing
co•pi•ous
cop•per
cop•per•head
cop•y
cop•y•ing
cop•y•right
cor•al
cord (sounds like "chord")
  Please tie this cord to the post.
cor•dial
cor•**dial**•i•ty
cor•dial•ly
cor•don
cor•du•roy
core
cork
cork•screw

corn
cor•ne•a
cor•ner
cor•ner•stone
cor•**net**
corn•flow•er
cor•nice
corn•meal
corn•row
corn•starch
co•**ro**•na
cor•o•nar•ies
cor•o•nar•y
cor•o•**na**•tion
cor•o•ner
cor•o•**net**
cor•po•ral
cor•po•**ra**•tion
corps
corpse
cor•pu•lence
cor•pu•lent
cor•pus•cle
cor•pus de•**lic**•ti
cor•**ral**
cor•**rect**
cor•**rec**•tion
cor•re•late
cor•re•lat•ing
cor•re•**la**•tion
cor•res•**pond**
cor•res•**pond**•ence
cor•res•**pond**•ent
cor•ri•dor

cor•**rode**
cor•**rod**•ing
cor•**ro**•sion
cor•**ro**•sive
cor•ru•gat•ed
cor•**rupt**
cor•**rupt**•i•ble
cor•**rup**•tion
cor•**sage**
cor•set
cos•**met**•ic
cos•mic
cos•mo•naut
cos•mo•**pol**•i•tan
cos•mos
cost
co-star
cost•ly
cos•tume
cot
cot•tage
cot•ton
cot•ton•mouth
cot•ton•tail
cot•ton•wood
couch
cou•gar
cough
could
could•n't
coun•cil (sounds like "counsel")
  The city council passed the law.

coun•sel (sounds like "council")

I will seek my grandfather's counsel.

coun•se•lor

count

count•down

coun•te•nance

coun•ter

coun•ter•**act**

coun•ter•**clock**•wise

coun•ter•feit

coun•ter•part

coun•ter•point

count•ess

coun•ties

coun•tries

coun•try

coun•try•side

coun•ty

cou•ple

cou•plet

cou•pling

cou•pon

cour•age

cou•**ra**•geous

cour•i•er

course (sounds like "coarse")

Math is her favorite course.

court

cour•te•ous

cour•te•sies

cour•te•sy

court•house

court•ly

court•room

court•ship

court•yard

cous•in

cove

cov•er

cov•er•age

cov•ered **wag**•on

co•vert

cov•et

cow

cow•ard

cow•ard•ice

cow•boy

cow•er

cow•girl

cow•hand

cow•hide

coy•**o**•te

also pronounced **coy**•ote

co•zi•ly

co•zy

crab

crab•by

crack

crack•down

crack•er

crack•le

crack•ling

cra•dle

craft

craft•i•er

craft•i•est

craft•i•ly

crafts•per•son

craft•y

crag

cram

crammed

cram•ming

cramp

cramped

cran•ber•ries

cran•ber•ry

crane

crank

crank•i•er

crank•i•est

crank•i•ness

crank•y

crash

crass

crate

cra•ter

crat•ing

cra•**vat**

crave

crav•ing

crawl

cray•fish

cray•on

craze

cra•zi•er

cra•zi•est

cra•zi•ly

cra•zi•ness

cra•zy

creak (sounds like "creek")

I oiled that noisy creak.

cream

cream•er•y

crease

creas•ing

cre•**ate**

cre•**at**•ing

cre•**a**•tion

cre•**a**•tive

cre•a•**tiv**•i•ty

crea•ture

crèche

cre•**den**•tials

cred•i•**bil**•i•ty

cred•i•ble

cred•it

cred•it **card**

creed

creek (sounds like "creak")

He fell into the creek and got all wet.

creep

creep•y

cre•mate

cre•**ma**•tion

Cre•ole

crepe

crepe pa•per

crept

cres•cent

crescent

crest

crest•fall•en

crev•ice

crew

crib

crick•et

cried

cries

crime

crim•i•nal

crim•i•**nol**•o•gist

crim•i•**nol**•o•gy

crim•son

cringe

cring•ing

crin•kle

crin•kling

crin•o•line

crip•ple

crip•pled

crip•pling

cri•ses

cri•sis

crisp

criss•cross

crit•ic

crit•i•cal

crit•i•cism

crit•i•cize

crit•i•ciz•ing

cri•**tique**

croak

cro•**chet**

crock•er•y

croc•o•dile

cro•cus

crook

crook•ed

crop

cropped

crop•ping

cro•**quet** (often confused with "croquette")

They're playing croquet on the lawn.

cro•**quette** (often confused with "croquet")

This fish croquette is delicious.

cross
cross•bow
cross•breed
cross-**coun**•try
cross-ex•**am**•ine
cross-**ref**•er•ence
cross•roads
cross•walk
cross•word **puz**•zle
crouch
croup
crou•ton
crow
crow•bar
crowd
crown
cru•cial
cru•ci•ble
cru•ci•fied
cru•ci•fies
cru•ci•**fix**•ion
cru•ci•fy
cru•ci•fy•ing
crude
cru•el
cru•el•ty
cruise
cruis•er
cruis•ing
crumb
crum•ble
crum•bling
crum•ple
crum•pling

crunch
cru•**sade**
cru•**sad**•er
cru•**sad**•ing
crush
crust
crus•**ta**•cean
crutch
cry

(cry)

cry•ing
crys•tal
crys•tal•line
crys•tal•lize
cub
cube
cub•ing
cu•bic
cu•bi•cle
cu•bit

cuck•oo
cu•cum•ber
cud
cud•dle
cud•dling
cue (sounds like
  "queue")
  *He forgot his cue in
  the play.*
cuff
cu•ing
cui•**sine**
cul-de-**sac**
cu•li•nar•y
cul•mi•nate
cul•mi•nat•ing
cul•mi•**na**•tion
cul•prit
cult
cul•ti•vate
cul•ti•vat•ing
cul•ti•**va**•tion
cul•tur•al
cul•ture
cul•tured
cum•ber•some
cun•ning
cum **lau**•de
cu•mu•late
cu•mu•lat•ing
cu•mu•**la**•tion
cu•mu•la•tive
cup
cup•board

cup•cake
cup•ful
Cu•pid
cupped
cup•ping
cur•a•ble
cu•rate
cu•ra•tor
  also pronounced
  cu•**ra**•tor
curb
curb•stone
curd
cur•dle
cur•dling
cure
cure-all
cur•few
cur•ing
cu•ri•**os**•i•ties
cu•ri•**os**•i•ty
cu•ri•ous
curl
cur•li•cue
curl•i•er
curl•i•est
curl•y
cur•rant (sounds like
  "current")
  *I made this currant
  jam myself.*

cur•ren•cy
cur•rent (sounds like
  "currant")
  *Electrical current runs
  through the wire.*
cur•**ric**•u•la
cur•**ric**•u•lum
cur•**ric**•u•lums
cur•ried
cur•ry
curse
curs•ing
cur•sor
cur•so•ry
cur•**tail**
cur•tain
curt
curt•sied
curt•sies
curt•sy
curve
curv•ing
cush•ion
cus•tard
cus•**to**•di•an
cus•to•dy
cus•tom
cus•tom•ar•y
cus•tom•er
cus•tom•ize
cus•tom-**made**

cut
cut•a•way
cute
cu•ti•cle
cut•lass
cut•le•ry
cut•ting
cy•ber•space
cy•cle
cy•cling
cy•clist
cy•clone
cy•clo•**ra**•ma
cyg•net
cyl•in•der
cym•bal (sounds like
  "symbol")
  *Strike that cymbal
  loudly.*
cyn•ic
cyn•i•cal
cyn•i•cism
cy•press
cyst
cy•to•plasm
czar (*or* **tsar**)
cza•**ri**•na (*or* tsa•**ri**•na)
Czech•o•slo•**va**•ki•a

dab
dabbed
dab·bing
dab·ble
dab·bling
dachs·hund
dad
dad·dies
dad·dy
dad·dy-**long**·legs
daf·fo·dil
daft
dag·ger
dai·ly
dain·ti·er
dain·ti·est
dain·ti·ly
dain·ti·ness
dain·ty
dair·ies
dair·y
dai·sies
dai·sy
dale
dal·lied
dal·lies
dal·ly
dal·ly·ing
dal·**ma**·tian
dam
dam·age
dam·aged

dam·ag·ing
Da·**mas**·cus
damp
damp·en
dam·sel
dance
danc·ing
dan·de·li·on
dan·di·er
dan·di·est
dan·druff
dan·dy
dan·ger
dan·ger·ous
dan·gle
dan·gling
dank
dap·ple
dap·pled
dap·pling
dare
dar·ing
dare·dev·il
dark
dark·en
dark·ness
dark·room
dar·ling
darn
dart
dash
dash·board

da·ta
da·ta·base
date
dat·ing
daugh·ter
daugh·ter-in-law
daugh·ters-in-law
daunt
daunt·ing
daunt·less
daw·dle
daw·dler
daw·dling
dawn
day
day·break
day care
day·dream
day·light
day·time
daze
daz·ing
daz·zle
daz·zling
dea·con
dead
dead·en
dead end
dead·line
dead·lock
dead·ly
deaf

deaf•en
deaf•en•ing
deaf•ness
deal
deal•er
dear
death
death•bed
death•ly
death•trap
de•ba•cle
de•bate
de•bat•ing
deb•it
deb•o•nair

debonair

de•bris
debt
debt•or
de•bug

de•but
  also pronounced
  de•but
deb•u•tante
dec•ade
dec•a•dence
dec•a•dent
de•caf•fein•at•ed
de•cal
de•cant•er
de•cap•i•tate
de•cap•i•tat•ing
de•cap•i•ta•tion
de•cath•lon
de•cay
de•ceased
de•ceit
de•ceit•ful
de•ceive
de•ceiv•ing
De•cem•ber
de•cen•cy
de•cent
de•cen•tral•ize
de•cep•tion
de•cep•tive
dec•i•bel
de•cide
de•cid•ed
de•cid•ing
de•cid•u•ous
dec•i•mal
de•ci•pher
de•ci•sion

de•ci•sive
deck
dec•la•ra•tion
Dec•la•ra•tion of
  In•de•pend•ence
de•clare
de•clar•ing
de•cline
de•clin•ing
de•code
de•cod•ing
de•com•pose
de•com•pos•ing
de•con•ges•tant
de•con•tam•i•nate
de•con•tam•i•nat•ing
de•con•tam•i•na•tion
dec•o•rate
dec•o•rat•ing
dec•o•ra•tion
de•cou•page
de•coy
de•crease (v.)
de•crease (n.)
de•creas•ing
de•cree
de•cree•ing
de•crep•it
de•cried
de•cries
de•cry
de•cry•ing
ded•i•cate
ded•i•cat•ing

ded•i•**ca**•tion
de•**duce**
de•**duc**•ing
de•**duct**
de•**duct**•i•ble
de•**duc**•tion
deed
deep
deep-seat•ed
deer
deer•skin
de•**face**
de•**fac**•ing
de•**feat**
de•**fect**
de•**fec**•tion
de•**fend**
de•**fend**•ant
de•**fense**
de•**fense**•less
de•**fen**•sive
de•**fer**
de•**ferred**
de•**fi**•ance
de•**fi**•ant
de•**fi**•cien•cies
de•**fi**•cien•cy
de•**fi**•cient
def•i•cit
de•**fied**
de•**fies**
de•**fine**
def•i•nite
def•i•**ni**•tion

de•**flate**
de•**flect**
de•for•est•**a**•tion
de•for•**ma**•tion
de•**formed**
de•**for**•mi•ty
de•**fraud**
de•**frost**
deft
de•**fuse**

defuse

de•**fus**•ing
de•**fy**
de•**gen**•er•ate
de•**gen**•er•at•ing
de•gen•er•**a**•tion
deg•ra•**da**•tion
de•**grade**
de•**grad**•ing
de•**gree**
de•**hy**•drate

de•**hy**•drat•ing
de•hy•**dra**•tion
de•i•ties
de•i•ty
de•**ject**•ed
de•**jec**•tion
Del•a•ware
de•**lay**
de•**lec**•ta•ble
del•e•gate
del•e•gat•ing
del•e•**ga**•tion
de•**lete**
de•**let**•ing
de•**lib**•er•ate
de•**lib**•er•at•ing
de•lib•er•**a**•tion
del•i•cate
del•i•ca•**tes**•sen
de•**li**•cious
de•**light**
de•**light**•ful
de•**light**•ful•ly
de•**lin**•quen•cy
de•**lin**•quent
de•**lir**•i•ous
de•**lir**•i•um
de•**liv**•er
de•**liv**•er•y
del•ta
de•**lude**
de•**lud**•ing
del•uge
de•**lu**•sion

de•**mand**
de•**mand**•ing
de•**mean**
de•**ment**•ed
de•**mer**•it
de•**mise**
dem•o
de•**moc**•ra•cies
de•**moc**•ra•cy
dem•o•crat
dem•o•**crat**•ic
Dem•o•**crat**•ic **Par**•ty
de•mo•**graph**•ics
de•**mol**•ish
dem•o•**li**•tion
de•mon
de•**mon**•ic
dem•on•strate
dem•on•strat•ing
dem•on•**stra**•tion
dem•**on**•stra•tive
de•**mor**•al•ized
den
de•**nied**
de•**nies**
den•im
Den•mark
de•**nom**•i•**na**•tion
de•**nom**•i•na•tor
de•**note**
de•**not**•ing
de•**nounce**
de•**noun**•ced
de•**nounc**•ing

dense
den•si•ty
dent
den•tal
den•tist
den•tist•ry
den•ture
de•**ny**
de•**ny**•ing
de•**o**•dor•ant
de•**o**•dor•ize
de•**part**
de•**part**•ment
de•part•**men**•tal
de•**par**•ture
de•**pend**
de•**pend**•a•**bil**•i•ty
de•**pend**•a•ble
de•**pend**•ence
de•**pend**•ent
de•**pict**
de•**plete**
de•**plet**•ing
de•**ple**•tion
de•**plor**•a•ble
de•**plore**
de•**plor**•ing
de•**ploy**
de•**ploy**•ment
de•**port**
de•**port**•ment
de•**pos**•it
de•**pos**•i•tor
de•**pos**•i•tor•y

de•pot
de•**praved**
de•**prav**•i•ty
de•**pre**•ci•ate
de•**pre**•ci•at•ing
de•**pressed**
de•**pres**•sion
dep•ri•**va**•tion
de•**prive**
de•**priv**•ing
depth
dep•u•tize
dep•u•ties
dep•u•ty
de•**rail**•ment
de•**ranged**
der•bies
der•by
der•e•lict
der•e•**lic**•tion
de•**ride**
de•**rid**•ing
de•**ri**•sion
de•**rive**
de•**riv**•ing
der•ma•**tol**•o•gist
der•ma•**tol**•o•gy
de•**rog**•a•to•ry
der•rick
de•**scend**
de•**scend**•ant
des•**cent**
de•**scribe**
de•**scrib**•ing

de•**scrip**•tion
de•**scrip**•tive
de•**seg**•re•gate
de•**seg**•re•gat•ing
de•**seg**•re•**ga**•tion
des•ert (n.)
The Sahara is the world's largest desert.
de•**sert** (v.) (sounds like "dessert")
A loyal friend won't desert you.
de•**serve**
de•**serv**•ing
de•**sign**
des•ig•nate
des•ig•nat•ing
des•ig•**na**•tion
de•**sign**•er
de•**sign**•ing
de•**sire**
de•**sir**•ing
desk
desk•top
des•o•late
des•o•**la**•tion
de•**spair**
des•per•**a**•do
des•per•ate
des•per•**a**•tion
de•**spise**
de•**spis**•ing
de•**spite**
de•**spond**•ent

des•pot
des•**pot**•ic
des•**pot**•ism
des•**sert** (sounds like "desert")
I'd like chocolate pudding for dessert.
des•ti•**na**•tion
des•tined
des•ti•ny
des•ti•tute
des•ti•**tu**•tion
de•**stroy**
de•**stroy**•er
de•**struct**•i•ble
des•**truc**•tive
de•**tach**
de•**tached**
de•**tach**•ment
de•**tail**
de•**tain**
de•**tect**
de•**tec**•tive
de•**tec**•tor
de•**ten**•tion
de•**ter**
de•**ter**•gent
de•**te**•ri•o•rate
de•**te**•ri•o•rat•ing
de•**te**•ri•o•**ra**•tion
de•**ter**•mi•**na**•tion
de•**ter**•mine
de•**ter**•mined
de•**ter**•min•ing

de•**test**
det•o•nate
det•o•nat•ing
det•o•**na**•tion
de•**tour**
de•**tract**
de•**trac**•tion
det•ri•**men**•tal
De•**troit**
deuce
de•**val**•u•ate
de•**val**•u•**a**•tion
de•**val**•ue
dev•as•tate
dev•as•tat•ing
dev•as•**ta**•tion
de•**vel**•op
de•**vel**•op•ing
de•**vel**•op•ment
de•vi•ate
de•vi•at•ing
de•vi•**a**•tion
de•**vice**
dev•il
dev•il•ish
de•vi•ous
de•**vise**
de•**vote**
de•**vot**•ed
de•**vot**•ing
de•**vo**•tion
de•**vour**
dew (sounds like "due")

The dew on the grass is slippery.

dew•y

dex•**ter**•i•ty

dex•ter•ous

di•a•**be**•tes

di•a•**bet**•ic

di•a•**bol**•ic

di•ag•**nose**

di•ag•**nos**•ing

di•ag•**no**•sis

di•ag•**nos**•tic

di•ag•nos•**ti**•cian

di•**ag**•o•nal

di•a•gram

di•al

di•a•lect

di•a•logue

di•**al**•y•sis

di•**am**•e•ter

dia•mond

di•a•per

di•a•phragm

di•ar•**rhe**•a

di•a•ries

di•a•ry

dice

dic•tate

dic•tat•ing

dic•**ta**•tion

dic•ta•tor

dic•ta•**to**•ri•al

dic•tion•ar•ies

dic•tion•ar•y

did

did•n't

die (sounds like "dye")

You won't die if you eat asparagus.

died (sounds like "dyed")

Lincoln died in 1865.

die•sel

di•et

di•e•tar•y

di•e•**tet**•ic

dif•fer•ence

dif•fer•ent

dif•fi•cult

dif•fi•cul•ty

dig

dig

di•**gest** (v.)

di•gest (n.)

di•**gest**•i•ble

di•**ges**•tion

dig•it

dig•it•al

dig•i•tize

dig•ni•fied

dig•ni•fies

dig•ni•ty

di•**gress**

di•**gres**•sion

di•**lap**•i•dat•ed

di•lap•i•**da**•tion

di•late

di•**lat**•ing

di•**la**•tion

di•**lem**•ma

dil•i•gence

dil•i•gent

di•**lute**

di•**lut**•ing

di•**lu**•tion

dim

dime

di•**men**•sion

di•**min**•ish

dimmed

dim•ming

dim•ple

din

dine

din•er

di•**nette**

ding•bat

din•ghy (often confused with "dingy")

Let's row to the island in the dinghy.

ding•i•er

ding•i•est

din•gy (often confused with "dinghy")

She painted the dark, dingy room white.

din•ing

din•ing **room**

din•ner

di•no•saur

di•o•cese

dip

di•**plo**•ma

di•**plo**•ma•cy

dip•lo•mat

dip•lo•**mat**•ic

dipped

dip•per

dip•ping

dire

di•**rect**

di•**rec**•tion

di•**rec**•tor

di•**rec**•to•ries

di•**rec**•to•ry

di•**ri**•gi•ble

dirt

dir•ti•er

dir•ti•est

dir•ti•ness

dir•ty

dis

dis•a•**bil**•i•ty

dis•**a**•ble

dis•**a**•bled

dis•ad•**van**•tage

dis•a•**gree**

dis•a•**gree**•a•ble

dis•a•**gree**•ing

dis•a•**gree**•ment

dis•ap•**pear**

dis•ap•**pear**•ance

dis•ap•**point**

dis•ap•**point**•ment

dis•ap•**prov**•al

dis•ap•**prove**

dis•ap•**prov**•ing

dis•**arm**

dis•**ar**•ma•ment

(**dirigible**)

dis•**as**•ter

dis•**as**•trous

dis•be•**lief**

dis•be•**lieve**

disc (or **disk**)

dis•**card**

dis•**charge** (v.)

dis•charge (n.)

dis•**charg**•ing

dis•**ci**•ple

dis•ci•pli•nar•y

dis•ci•pline

dis•ci•plin•ing

disc jock•ey

dis•**claim**

dis•**claim**•er

dis•**close**

dis•**clos**•ing

dis•**clo**•sure

dis•co

dis•**com**•fort

dis•con•**nect**

dis•con•**tent**•ed

dis•con•**tin**•ue

dis•con•**tin**•u•ing

dis•cord

dis•count

dis•**cour**•age

dis•**cour**•age•ment

dis•**cour**•ag•ing

dis•**cov**•er

dis•**creet**

dis•**crim**•i•nate

dis•**crim**•i•nat•ing

dis•crim•i•**na**•tion

dis•cus (often confused with "discuss")

He threw the discus in the Olympics.

dis•**cuss** (often confused with "discus")

Let's discuss this matter later.

dis•**cus**•sion

dis•**ease**

dis•**fig**•ure

dis•**grace**

dis•**grace**•ful

dis•**grac**•ing

dis•**grun**•tled

dis•**guise**

dis•**guis**•ing

dis•**gust**•ing

dish

dish•es

di•**shev**•eled

dis•**hon**•est

dis•**hon**•or

dis•**hon**•or•able

dish•wash•er

dis•il•**lu**•sion

dis•in•**fect**

dis•in•**fect**•ant

dis•**in**•te•grate

dis•**in**•te•grat•ing

dis•**in**•te•**gra**•tion

dis•**in**•ter•est•ed

dis•**joint**•ed

disk or **disc**

dis•**like**

dis•**lo**•cate

   also pronounced **dis**•lo•cate

dis•lo•**ca**•tion

dis•**lodge**

dis•**lodg**•ing

dis•mal

dis•**man**•tle

dis•**mayed**

dis•**miss**

dis•**miss**•al

dis•**mount**

dis•o•**be**•di•ent

dis•o•**bey**

dis•**or**•der•ly

dis•**or**•gan•ized

dis•**own**

dis•**patch**

dis•**pel**

dis•**pen**•sa•ble

dis•**pen**•sa•ries

dis•**pen**•sa•ry

dis•**pense**

dis•**place**

dis•**place**•ment

dis•**plac**•ing

dis•**play**

dis•**please**

dis•**pleas**•ing

dis•**pos**•a•ble

dis•**pos**•al

dis•**pose**

dis•po•**si**•tion

dis•**prove**

dis•**prov**•ing

dis•**pute**

dis•**put**•ing

dis•qual•i•fi•**ca**•tion

dis•**qual**•i•fied

dis•**qual**•i•fies

dis•**qual**•i•fy

dis•re•**gard**

dis•**rep**•u•ta•ble

dis•res•**pect**

dis•res•**pect**•ful

dis•res•**pect**•ful•ly

dis•**rupt**

dis•**rup**•tion

dis•sat•is•**fac**•tion

dis•**sat**•is•fied

dis•**sat**•is•fies

dis•**sat**•is•fy

dis•**sect**

dis•**sec**•tion

dis•**sem**•i•nate

dis•**sem**•i•nat•ing

dis•sem•i•**na**•tion

dis•**sen**•sion

dis•**sent**

dis•**serv**•ice

dis•si•dent

dis•**solve**

dis•**solv**•ing

dis•**suade**

dis•**suad**•ing

dis•tance

dis•tant

dis•**taste**

dis•**taste**•ful

dis•**tem**•per

dis•**till**

dis•til•**la**•tion

dis•**till**•er•y

dis•**tinct**

dis•**tinc**•tion

dis•**tinc**•tive

dis•**tin**•guish

dis•**tin**•guish•a•ble

dis•**tin**•guished

dis•**tort**

dis•**tor**•tion

dis•**tract**

dis•**trac**•tion

dis•**tress**

dis•**trib**•ute

dis•**trib**•ut•ing

dis•tri•**bu**•tion

dis•**trib**•u•tor

dis•trict

dis•**trust**

dis•**turb**

dis•**turb**•ance

dis•**use**

ditch

dit•to

dive

div•er

di•**verse**

di•**ver**•sion

di•**ver**•si•ty

di•**vert**

di•**vide**

di•**vid**•ed

div•i•dend

di•**vid**•ing

di•**vine**

div•ing

di•**vis**•i•ble

di•**vi**•sion

di•**vi**•sor

di•**vorce**

di•**vorc**•ing

di•**vulge**

di•**vulg**•ing

diz•zi•er

diz•zi•est

diz•zi•ness

diz•zy

do

Do•ber•man **pin**•scher

doc•ile

dock

dock•et

dock•yard

doc•tor

doc•tor•ate

doc•trine

doc•u•dra•ma

doc•u•ment

doc•u•**men**•ta•ries

doc•u•**men**•ta•ry

dodge

dodg•ing

doe (sounds like "dough")

Look at the beautiful doe in the woods.

does

does•n't

dog

dog•house

dog•ma

dog•**mat**•ic

dog•wood

doi•lies

doi•ly

dole

doll

dol•lar

dol•phin

dome

do•**mes**•tic

do•**mes**•ti•cate

do•mes•ti•**ca**•tion

dom•i•nant

dom•i•nate

dom•i•nat•ing

dom•i•**na**•tion

do•**min**•ion

dom•i•no

dom•i•noes (*or* **dom**•i•nos)

don

do•nate

do•**na**•tion

done

don•key
donned
don•ning
do•nor
don't
do•nut (*or* **dough**•nut)
doo•dle
doo•dling
doom
dooms•day
door
door•bell
door•knob
door•man
door•step
door•way
dope
dor•mant
dor•mi•to•ries
dor•mi•to•ry
dos•age
dose
dot
dote
dot•ted
dot•ting
dou•ble
dou•ble-**cross**
dou•ble-**head**•er
doubt
dough (sounds like "doe")
 I knead the dough to make bread.

dough•nut (*or* **do**•nut)
dove (rhymes with "love")
 A dove is a bird.
dove (rhymes with "stove")
 She dove into the pool.
down
down•cast
down•load

downpour

down•pour
down•right
downs
down•size
down•stairs (adv. and n.)
down•stairs (adj.)
down•stream
Down syn•drome (also called **Down's** syndrome)

down•town
doze
doz•en
doz•ing
drab
draft
drag
drag•on
drag•on•flies
drag•on•fly
drain
drain•age
drained
dra•ma
dra•**mat**•ic
dra•**mat**•i•cal•ly
dram•a•tize
drape
drap•ing
dras•tic
draw
draw•back
draw•bridge
drawer
 The socks are in the top drawer.
draw•er
 The talented drawer drew lovely pictures.
drawl
drawn
draw•string
dread
dread•ful

dread·locks
dream
dream·y
drear·y
dredge
dredg·ing
dregs
drench
dress
dress·er
dress·ing
drew
drib·ble
drib·bling
dried
dri·er (sounds like "dryer")
This shirt is drier than the other one.
dries
dri·est
drift
drift·wood
drill
dri·ly
drink
drip
dripped
drip·ping
drip·pings
drive
drive-in
driv·en
drive·way

driv·ing
driz·zle
driz·zling
driz·zly
drone
dron·ing
drool
droop
droop·ed
droop·ing
drop
dropped
drop·ping
drought
drove
drown
drows·i·er
drows·i·est
drow·si·ness
drow·sy
drudge
drudg·er·y
drug
drugged
drug·gist
drug·store
drum
drummed
drum·mer
drum·ming
drum·stick
drunk
dry

dry cell
dry-clean
dry·er (sounds like "drier")
Put the wet clothes into the dryer.
dry·ing
dual (sounds like "duel")
My new car has dual exhaust pipes.
du·bi·ous
duch·ess
duck
duct
dud
due (sounds like "dew")
The homework is due today.

drummer

duel (sounds like "dual")

The duel was fought at daybreak.

du•et

dug•out

duke

dull

dumb

dumb•bell

dumb•found•ed

dum•my

dump

dune

dun•ga•**ree**

dun•geon

du•plex

du•pli•cate

du•pli•cat•ing

du•pli•ca•tion

du•pli•ca•tor

du•ra•**bil**•i•ty

du•ra•ble

du•**ra**•tion

dur•ing

dusk

dusk•y

dust

dust•bin

dust•pan

dust•y

du•ties

du•ti•ful

du•ty

dwarf

dwarf•ish

dwarfs (*or* **dwarves**)

dwell

dwell•ing

dwin•dle

dwin•dling

dye (sounds like "die")

She will dye her shoes to match her dress.

dyed (sounds like "died")

She dyed her hair blonde.

dye•ing (sounds like "dying")

He's dyeing his shirt green.

dy•ing (sounds like "dyeing")

She's dying to meet the new boy.

dy•**nam**•ic

dy•na•mite

dy•na•mo

dy•na•mos

dy•nas•ties

dy•nas•ty

dys•**lex**•i•a

dys•**lex**•ic

dys•en•ter•y

each
ea•ger
ea•ger•ly
ea•gle
ear
ear•ache
ear•drum
ear•li•er
ear•li•est
ear•ly
ear•muffs
earn (sounds like "urn")

How much will I earn for this job?

ear•nest
ear•phone
ear•ring
ear•shot
earth
earth•bound
earth•i•ness
earth•ling
earth•ly
earth•quake
earth•shak•ing
earth•worm
earth•y
ease
ea•sel
eas•i•er
eas•i•est

eas•i•ly
eas•i•ness
eas•ing
east
East•er
eas•y
eas•y•go•ing
eat
eat•a•ble
eaves
eaves•drop
eaves•drop•ping
ebb
eb•on•y
ec•cen•tric
ec•cen•tric•i•ty
ech•o
ech•oed
ech•oes
ech•o•ing
e•clipse
e•clips•ing
ec•o•log•i•cal
e•col•o•gist
e•col•o•gy
e•co•nom•i•cal
e•co•nom•ics
e•con•o•mist
e•con•o•mize
e•con•o•my
ec•o•sys•tem
ec•sta•sy

ec•stat•ic
Ec•ua•dor
ec•ze•ma
ed•dies
ed•dy
E•den
edge
edge•wise
edg•ing
edg•y
ed•i•ble
ed•i•fice
ed•it
ed•it•ing
e•di•tion
ed•i•tor
ed•i•to•ri•al
ed•i•to•ri•al•ize
ed•u•cate
ed•u•cat•ing
ed•u•ca•tion
ed•u•ca•tion•al•ly
ed•u•ca•tor
eel
ee•rie
ee•ri•er
ee•ri•est
ee•ri•ness
ef•fect
ef•fec•tive
ef•fer•ves•cence
ef•fer•ves•cent

ef•**fi**•cien•cy

ef•**fi**•cient

ef•fi•gy

ef•fort

egg

egg•head

egg•nog

egg•plant

egg•shell

e•go

e•go•**cen**•tric

e•go•tism

e•go•tist

e•go•**tis**•tic

e•gret

E•gypt

Eif•fel **Tow**•er

eight (sounds like "ate")

The cat had eight kittens.

eigh•**teen**

eight•i•eth

eight•y

Ein•stein

Ei•sen•how•er

ei•ther

e•**ject**

e•**jec**•tion

e•**lab**•o•rate

e•**lab**•o•rat•ing

e•lab•o•**ra**•tion

e•**lapse**

e•**laps**•ing

e•**las**•tic

e•las•**tic**•i•ty

el•bow

el•der

el•der•ber•ries

el•der•ber•ry

eld•er•ly

eld•est

e•**lect**

e•**lec**•tion

e•**lec**•tive

e•**lec**•tor•ate

e•**lec**•tric

e•**lec**•tri•cal•ly

e•lec•**tri**•cian

e•lec•**tric**•ity

e•lec•tri•fi•**ca**•tion

e•**lec**•tri•fied

e•**lec**•tri•fies

e•**lec**•tri•fy

elf

e•**lec**•tri•fy•ing

e•**lec**•tro•cute

e•lec•tro•**cu**•tion

e•**lec**•trode

e•**lec**•**trol**•y•sis

e•**lec**•tro•lyte

e•lec•tro•**mag**•net

e•lec•tro•**mag**•net•ism

e•**lec**•tron

e•lec•**tron**•ic

e•lec•**tron**•ics

el•e•gance

el•e•gant

el•e•gies

el•e•gy

el•e•ment

el•e•**men**•tal

el•e•**men**•ta•ry

el•e•phant

el•e•**phan**•tine

el•e•vate

el•e•vat•ing

el•e•**va**•tion

el•e•va•tor

e•**lev**•en

e•**lev**•enth

elf

el•i•gi•**bil**•i•ty

el•**i**•gi•ble

e•**lim**•i•nate

e•**lim**•i•nat•ing

e•lim•i•**na**•tion

e•**lite**

e•**lix**•ir

E•liz•a•**be**•than
elk
el•**lipse**
elm
e•**lope**
e•**lope**•ment
e•**lop**•ing
el•o•quence
el•o•quent
else
else•where
e•**lude** (sounds like "allude")

How long can the thief elude the police?

e•**lu**•sive
elves
e•**man**•ci•pate
e•**man**•ci•pat•ing
e•man•ci•**pa**•tion
e•**man**•ci•pa•tor
em•**balm**
em•**balm**•er
em•**bank**•ment
em•**bar**•go
em•**bar**•goes
em•**bark**
em•bar•**ka**•tion
em•**bar**•rass
em•**bar**•rass•ment
em•bas•sies
em•bas•sy
em•**bed**
em•**bel**•lish

em•**bel**•lish•ment
em•bers
em•**bez**•zle
em•**bez**•zler
em•**bit**•tered
em•blem
em•**bod**•ied
em•**bod**•ies
em•**bod**•i•ment
em•**bod**•y
em•**boss**
em•**brace**
em•**brace**•a•ble
em•**brac**•ing
em•**broi**•der
em•**broi**•der•y
em•bry•o
em•bry•os
em•er•ald
e•**mer**•gen•cy
em•i•grate
em•i•grat•ing
em•i•**gra**•tion
e•**mis**•sion
e•**mit**
e•**mit**•ted
e•**mit**•ting
e•**mote**
e•**mot**•ing
e•**mo**•tion
e•**mo**•tion•al
e•**mo**•tion•al•ism
e•**mo**•tion•al•ly
em•pa•thy

em•per•or
em•pha•sis
em•pha•size
em•pha•siz•ing
em•**phat**•ic
em•pire
em•**ploy**
em•**ploy**•ee
em•**ploy**•er

embrace

em•**ploy**•ment
em•press
emp•ti•ed
emp•ti•ness
emp•ty
emp•ty•ing
em•u•late
em•u•lat•ing
en•**a**•ble
en•**a**•bling
e•**nam**•el

e•**nam**•eled
en•**chant**
en•**chant**•ed
en•**chant**•ing
en•**chant**•ress
en•chil•**a**•da
en•**cir**•cle
en•**cir**•cling
en•**close**
en•**clos**•ing
en•**clo**•sure
en•**com**•pass
en•**core**
en•**coun**•ter
en•**cour**•age
en•**cour**•age•ment
en•**cour**•ag•ing
en•cy•clo•**pe**•di•a
end
en•**dan**•ger
en•**dan**•gered
en•**deav**•or
en•dive
end•less
en•**dor**•phin
en•**dorse**
en•**dorse**•ment
en•**dors**•ing
en•**dow**
en•**dow**•ment
en•**dure**
en•**dur**•ing
en•e•mies
en•e•my

en•er•**get**•ic
en•er•gize
en•er•gy
en•**force**
en•**force**•a•ble
en•**force**•ment
en•**forc**•ing
en•**gage**
en•**gage**•ment
en•**gag**•ing
en•gine
en•gi•**neer**
Eng•land
Eng•lish
en•**grave**
en•**grav**•ing
en•**gross**
en•**gross**•ing
en•**hance**
en•**hance**•ment
en•**hanc**•ing
e•**nig**•ma
en•ig•**mat**•ic
en•ig•**mat**•i•cal•ly
en•**joy**
en•**joy**•a•ble
en•**joy**•ment
en•**large**
en•**large**•ment
en•**larg**•ing
en•**light**•en
en•**light**•en•ment
en•**list**
en•**list**•ment

e•**nor**•mi•ty
e•**nor**•mous
e•**nough**
en•**rage**
en•**rag**•ing
en•**rich**
en•**rich**•ment
en•**roll**
en•**roll**•ment
en•route
en•**sem**•ble
en•**slave**
en•**slave**•ment
en•**tan**•gle
en•**tan**•gle•ment
en•ter
en•ter•prise
en•ter•pris•ing
en•ter•**tain**
en•ter•**tain**•ment
en•**thrall**
en•**thu**•si•asm
en•thu•si•**as**•tic
en•thu•si•**as**•ti•cal•ly
en•**tice**
en•**tice**•ment
en•**tic**•ing
en•**tire**
en•**tire**•ty
en•**trance**
en•**trap**
en•**trap**•ment
en•**trapped**
en•tre•pre•**neur**

en•tries
en•**trust**
en•try
e•**nun**•ci•ate
e•**nun**•ci•at•ing
e•nun•ci•**a**•tion
en•**vel**•op (v.)
en•ve•lope (n.)
en•**vel**•op•ing
en•vi•a•ble
en•vi•ous
en•**vi**•ron•ment
en•vi•ron•**men**•tal
en•vied
en•vies
en•vy
en•zyme
e•on
ep•ic
ep•i•cen•ter
ep•i•cure
ep•i•cu•**re**•an
ep•i•**dem**•ic
ep•i•**glot**•tis
ep•i•lep•sy
ep•i•logue
E•pis•co•**pa**•li•an
ep•i•sode
ep•i•taph
e•**pit**•o•mize
ep•och
e•qual
e•**qual**•i•ty
e•qual•ize

e•**quate**
e•**quat**•ing
e•**qua**•tion
e•**qua**•tor
e•qua•**to**•ri•al
e•**ques**•tri•an
e•qui•**lat**•er•al
e•qui•**lib**•ri•um
e•qui•nox
e•**quip**
e•**quip**•ment
e•**quipped**
e•**quip**•ping
e•**quiv**•a•lent
e•ra
e•**rase**
e•**ras**•er
e•**ras**•ing
e•**rect**
e•**rec**•tor
er•mine
e•**rode**
e•**rod**•ing
e•**ro**•sion
err
er•rand
er•**rat**•ic
erred
err•ing
er•ror
e•**rupt**
e•**rup**•tion
es•ca•late
es•ca•lat•ing

es•ca•la•tor
es•**cape**
es•**cap**•ing
es•**cort** (v.)
es•cort (n.)
Es•ki•mo
Es•ki•mos
e•**soph**•a•gus
es•**pe**•cial•ly
Es•pe•**ran**•to
es•pi•o•nage
es•pla•nade
es•say
es•say•ist
es•**sen**•tial
es•**tab**•lish
es•**tab**•lish•ment
es•ti•mate
es•ti•mat•ing
es•tu•ar•y
etc.
etch
e•**ter**•nal
e•**ter**•ni•ty
e•ther
eth•ics
E•thi•**o**•pi•a
eth•nic
et•i•quette
et•y•**mol**•o•gist
et•y•**mol**•o•gy
eu•ca•**lyp**•tus
eu•lo•gies
eu•lo•gy

eu•phe•mism
Eu•rope
Eu•ro•**pe**•an
eu•tha•**na**•sia
e•**vac**•u•ate
e•**vac**•u•at•ing
e•vac•u•**a**•tion
e•**vade**
e•**vad**•ing
e•**val**•u•ate
e•**val**•u•at•ing
e•val•u•**a**•tion
e•van•**gel**•i•cal
e•**van**•ge•list
e•**vap**•o•rate
e•**vap**•o•rat•ing
e•vap•o•**ra**•tion
eve
e•ven
eve•ning
e•**vent**
e•**ven**•tu•al
e•**ven**•tu•al•ly
ev•er
ev•er•glade
ev•er•green
ev•er•**last**•ing
eve•ry
eve•ry•bod•y
eve•ry•day
eve•ry•one
eve•ry•thing
eve•ry•where
e•**vict**

e•**vic**•tion
ev•i•dence
ev•i•dent
e•vil
e•vil-**mind**•ed
e•**voke**
e•**vok**•ing
ev•o•**lu**•tion
e•**volve**
e•**volv**•ing
ewe (sounds like "you")
   *A ewe is a female
   sheep.*

(**ewe**)

ex•**act**
ex•**act**•ly
ex•**ag**•ger•ate
ex•**ag**•ger•at•ing
ex•**ag**•ger•**a**•tion
ex•**am**

ex•am•in•**a**•tion
ex•**am**•ine
ex•**am**•in•ing
ex•**am**•ple
ex•**as**•per•ate
ex•**as**•per•at•ing
ex•as•per•**a**•tion
ex•ca•vate
ex•ca•vat•ing
ex•ca•**va**•tion
ex•**ceed**
ex•**cel**
ex•**celled**
ex•cel•lence
ex•cel•lent
ex•**cel**•ling
ex•**cept** (sounds like
   "accept")
   *I like every dish
   except the last one.*
ex•**cep**•tion
ex•**cep**•tion•al
ex•**cerpt** (v.)
ex•cerpt (n.)
ex•cess
   also pronounced
   ex•**cess**
ex•**ces**•sive
ex•**change**
ex•**chang**•ing
ex•**cite**
ex•**cite**•ment
ex•**cit**•ing
ex•**claim**

ex•cla•**ma**•tion
ex•**clude**
ex•**clud**•ing
ex•**clu**•sion
ex•**clu**•sive
ex•**crete**
ex•**cru**•ci•at•ing
ex•**cur**•sion
ex•**cuse**
ex•**cus**•ing
ex•e•cute
ex•e•cut•ing
ex•e•**cu**•tion
ex•**ec**•u•tive
ex•**empt**
ex•er•cise
ex•er•cis•ing
ex•hal•**a**•tion
ex•**hale**
ex•**hal**•ing
ex•**haust**
ex•**haus**•ting
ex•**hib**•it
ex•hi•**bi**•tion
ex•**hil**•a•rat•ing
ex•ile
ex•**ist**
ex•**ist**•ence
ex•it
ex•o•dus
ex•**on**•er•ate
ex•**or**•bi•tant
ex•or•cise
ex•or•cism

ex•o•**skel**•e•ton
ex•**ot**•ic
ex•**pand**
ex•**panse**
ex•**pect**
ex•pec•**ta**•tion
ex•pe•dite
ex•pe•dit•ing
ex•pe•**di**•tion
ex•**pel**
ex•**pelled**
ex•**pense**
ex•**pen**•sive
ex•**pe**•ri•ence
ex•**per**•i•ment
ex•**per**•i•**men**•tal
ex•pert
ex•pi•**ra**•tion
ex•**pire**
ex•**pir**•ing

ex•**plain**
ex•**plan**•a•tion
ex•**plic**•it
ex•**plode**
ex•**plod**•ing
ex•ploit (n.)
ex•**ploit** (v.)
ex•plo•**ra**•tion
ex•**plore**
ex•**plor**•er
ex•**plor**•ing
ex•**plo**•sion
ex•**plo**•sive
ex•**po**•nent
ex•port (n.)
ex•**port** (v.)
  also pronounced
  ex•port
ex•por•**ta**•tion
ex•**pose**
ex•**pos**•ing
ex•**po**•sure
ex•**press**
ex•**pres**•sion
ex•**pres**•sive
ex•**press**•way
ex•**qui**•site
ex•**tend**
ex•**ten**•sion
ex•**ten**•sive
ex•**tent**
ex•**te**•ri•or
ex•**ter**•mi•nate
ex•**ter**•nal

exhaust

ex•**tinct**
ex•**tinc**•tion
ex•**tin**•guish
ex•tra
ex•**tract** (n.)
ex•**tract** (v.)
ex•**traor**•di•nar•y

ex•tra•ter•**res**•tri•al
ex•**trav**•a•gance
ex•**trav**•a•gant
ex•**treme**
ex•tro•vert
ex•**u**•ber•ant
eye

eye•ball
eye•brow
eye•lash
eye•lid
eye•sight
eye•tooth
eye•**wit**•ness

fa·ble
fab·ric
fab·ri·cate
fab·ri·**ca**·tion
fab·u·lous
fa·**cade**
face
fa·**cil**·i·tate
fa·**cil**·i·tat·ing
fa·**cil**·i·ties
fa·**cil**·i·ty
fac·**sim**·i·le
fact
fac·tor
fac·to·ries
fac·to·ry
fac·tu·al
fac·ul·ties
fac·ul·ty
fad
fade
fad·ing
Fahr·en·heit
fail
fail·ure
faint (sounds like "feint")
We barely heard the faint sound.
fair
fair·ground
fair·ies

fair·ly
fair·ness
fair·y
faith
faith·ful
faith·ful·ly
fake
fak·ing
fa·**la**·fel
fal·con
fall
fall·out
false
false·hood
fal·ter
fame
fa·**mil**·iar
fa·mil·**iar**·i·ty
fam·i·lies
fam·i·ly
fam·ine
fam·ished
fa·mous
fan
fa·**nat**·ic
fan·ci·er
fan·ci·est
fan·ci·ness
fan·cy
fang
fan·ta·sies
fan·ta·size

fan·ta·siz·ing
fan·**tas**·tic
fan·ta·sy
fan·zine
far
far·a·**way**
farce
fare
fare·**well**
far-fetched
farm
far·**sight**·ed
far·ther
fas·ci·nate
fas·ci·nat·ing
fas·ci·**na**·tion
fas·cism
fas·cist
fash·ion
fash·ion·a·ble
fast
fas·ten
fas·ten·er
fas·**tid**·i·ous
fat
fa·tal
fa·**tal**·i·ties
fa·**tal**·i·ty
fate
fate·ful
fa·ther
fath·om

fa•**tigue**
fat•ter
fat•test
fau•cet
fault
fau•na
fa•vor
fa•vor•a•ble
fa•vor•ite
fa•vor•it•ism
fawn
fax
fear
fear•ful
fear•less
fea•si•ble
feast
feat
feath•er
fea•ture
Feb•ru•ar•y
fed
fed•er•al
fed•er•**a**•tion
fee
fee•ble
feed
feed•back
feel
feet
feign
feint (sounds like
  "faint")
  The troops made a

*feint on one side of
the island before
actually attacking the
other side.*
feist•y
fe•line

(**feline**)

fell
fel•low
felt
fe•male
fem•i•nine
fem•i•nist
fence
fenc•ing
fend
fend•er
fer•**ment**
fern
fe•**ro**•cious
fe•**roc**•i•ty

fer•ret
Fer•ris **wheel**
fer•ry
fer•tile
fer•ti•li•**za**•tion
fer•ti•lize
fer•ti•liz•er
fer•ti•liz•ing
fer•vent
fes•ti•val
fes•tive
fes•**tiv**•ity
fetch
fetch•ing
fet•tuc•**ci**•ne
fe•tus
feud
feu•dal•ism
fe•ver
few
fez
fi•an•**cé** (sounds like
  "fi•an•cée")
  *Her fiancé is
  Mr. Jones.*
fi•an•**cée** (sounds like
  "fi•an•cé")
  *He gave his fiancée
  a ring.*
fib
fibbed
fib•bing
fi•ber
fi•ber•glass

fick•le
fic•tion
fid•dle
fid•dler
fid•dling
fidg•et
field
field•er
fiend
fierce
fier•y
fi•**es**•ta
fifth
fig
fight
fig•ure
fil•a•ment
file
fill
fil•let
  also pronounced
  fil•**let**
fil•ling
fil•ly
film
fil•ter
filth
fil•**tra**•tion
fin
fi•nal
fi•**na**•le
fi•nal•ist
fi•nal•ize
fi•nal•ly

fi•nance
fi•**nan**•cial
fi•**nanc**•ing
finch
find
find•ing
fine
fin•er
fin•est
fin•ger
fin•ger•nail
fin•ger•print
fin•ick•y
fin•ish
fi•nite
Fin•land
Fin•nish
fir
fire
fire•arm
fire•crack•er
fire ex•**tin**•guish•er

fire extinguisher

fire•fight•er
fire•flies
fire•fly
fire•house
fire•man
fire•place
fire•proof
fire•side
fire•trap
fire•wood
fire•works
firm
first
first•hand
first-rate
fish
fish•er•man
fish•er•y
fish•ing rod
fish•y
fis•sion
fist
fit
fit•ness
fit•ting
five
fix
fix•a•tion
fix•ture
fizz
fiz•zle
fjord (*or* fiord)
flab
flab•ber•gast•ed

flag
flag•pole
flair
flak
flake
flam•**boy**•ant
flame
fla•**min**•go
fla•**min**•gos (*or* fla•**min**•goes)
flam•ma•ble
flank
flan•nel
flap
flap•jack
flare
flash
flash•back
flash•light
flash•y
flask
flat
flat•bed
flat•car
flat•ter
flaunt (sometimes confused with "flout")
She shouldn't flaunt her A+ test score.
fla•vor
flaw
flax
flea
fleck

fledg•ling
flee
fleece
fleet
fleet•ing
Flem•ish
flesh
flew
flex
flex•i•ble
flex•time
flick
flick•er
flight
flim•sy
flinch
fling
flint
flip
flip•pant
flip•per
flirt
float
flock
flog
flood
flood•light
floor
flop
flop•py
flo•ra
flo•ral
Flor•i•da

flo•rist
floss
flot•sam
floun•der
flour
flour•ish
flout (sometimes confused with "flaunt")
To flout the dress code, come barefoot to class.
flow
flow•chart
flow•er
flu
fluc•tu•ate
flu•en•cy
flu•ent
fluff
fluff•y
flu•id
fluke
fluo•**res**•cent
fluor•i•date
fluor•i•dat•ing
fluor•i•**da**•tion
fluor•ide
fluo•rine
flur•ry
flush
flushed
flus•ter
flute

flut•ter
fly
fly•catch•er
foal
foam
fo•cus
fod•der
foe
fog
fog•horn
foil
fold
fold•er
fo•li•age
folk
folk•lore
folk•tale
fol•lies
fol•low
fol•low•ing
fol•ly
fond
fon•dle
font
food
food proc•es•sor
fool
fool•ish
fool•proof
foot
foot•ball
foot•hill
foot•ing

foot•lights
foot•note
foot•print
foot•step
for
for•age
for•**bid**
for•**bid**•den
for•**bid**•ding
force
for•ceps
forc•ing
ford
fore•cast
fore•fa•ther
fore•fin•ger
fore•ground
fore•head
for•eign
fore•most
fo•**ren**•sic
fore•run•ner
fore•**see**
fore•sight
for•est
for•est **rang**•er
for•**ev**•er
fore•word
for•feit
for•**gave**
forge
forg•er
for•ger•y

for•**get**
for•**get**•ful
for•**get**•ting
for•**give**
for•**giv**•en
for•**give**•ness
for•**giv**•ing
for•**got**
for•**got**•ten
fork
fork•lift
for•**lorn**
form
for•mal
for•**mal**•i•ty
for•**mal**•ly (often
   confused with
   "formerly")
   Please dress
   formally.
for•mat
for•**ma**•tion
for•mer
for•mer•ly (often
   confused with
   "formally")
   He formerly lived
   in Spain.
for•mi•da•ble
form•less
for•mu•la
for•**sake**
for•**sak**•en
for•**sak**•ing

fort (sounds like "forte")
The old fort still had cannons.

forte (sounds like "fort"; also pronounced **for**•te)
Her forte is tennis.

forth

forth•com•ing

for•ti•fi•**ca**•tion

for•ti•fied

for•ti•fies

for•tl•fy

fort•night

for•tress

for•tu•nate

for•tu•nate•ly

for•tune

fo•rum

for•ward

fos•sil

fos•ter

fought

foul (sounds like "fowl")
That ball was foul.

found

foun•**da**•tion

found•ry

foun•tain

four

fourth

fowl (sounds like "foul")
A pheasant is a fowl.

fox

fox•es

foy•er

frac•tal

frac•tion

frac•ture

frag•ile

frag•ment

fra•grance

fra•grant

frail

frame

frame•work

fran•chise

frank

frank•fur•ter

frankfurter

fran•tic

fraud

fray

freak

freck•le

free

free•dom

free•lance

free-range

free•way

freeze

freeze-dried

free•zer

freez•ing

freight

freight•er

French

French fries

French horn

fren•zied

fren•zy

fre•quen•cies

fre•quen•cy

fre•quent

fres•co

fres•coes (*or* **fres**•cos)

fresh

fresh•man

fresh•wa•ter

fret

fric•tion

Fri•day

fridge

fried

friend
friend•li•ness
friend•ly
friend•ship
fright
fright•en
fright•ful
frig•id
frill
fringe
Fris•bee
frisk
frisk•y
frit•**ta**•ta
frit•ter
friv•o•lous
frog
frol•ic
from
front
fron•tier
frost
frost•bite
frost•ing
frost•y
froth
frown
froze
fro•zen
fru•gal
fruit
fruit•ful

fruit•less
frus•trate
fry
fry•ing
fudge
fu•el

frog

fu•gi•tive
ful•crum
ful•**fill**
full
fum•ble
fume
fun
func•tion
func•tion•al
fund
fun•da•**men**•tal
fu•ner•al

fun•gus
fun•nel
fun•ni•er
fun•ni•est
fun•ny
fur
fu•ri•ous
fur•lough
fur•nace
fur•nish
fur•ni•ture
fur•ry
fur•ther
fur•ther•more
fu•ry
fuse
fu•se•lage
fu•sion
fuss
fuss•i•er
fuss•i•est
fuss•y
fu•tile
fu•til•i•ty
fu•ton
fu•ture
fuzz
fuzz•i•er
fuzz•i•est
fuzz•i•ness
fuzz•y

gab

gad•get

gag

gagged

gag•ging

gain

gait (sounds like "gate")

In those shoes, you walk with a clumsy gait.

ga•la

gal•ax•ies

gal•ax•y

gale

gal•lant

gall•blad•der

gal•ler•ies

gal•ler•y

gal•ley

gal•lon

gal•lop

gal•ore

gal•va•nize

gam•ble

gam•bling

game

gan•der

gang

gang•plank

gan•grene

also pronounced
gan•grene

gang•ster

gang•way

gap

gap•ing

ga•**rage**

gar•bage

gar•ble

gar•bled

gar•den

gar•den•er

gar•**de**•nia

gar•gle

gar•gling

gar•land

gar•lic

gar•ment

gar•net

gar•nish

gar•ter

gas

gash

gas•o•hol

gas•o•**line**

gasp

gate (sounds like "gait")

The goat ran through the open gate.

gate•way

gath•er

gaud•y

gauge (rhymes with "cage")

gaunt

gauze

gave

gav•el

gay

gaze

ga•**zelle**

ga•zet•**teer**

gaz•ing

gear

gear•shift

geese

Gei•ger **coun**•ter

gel

ge•**la**•ti

gel•a•tin (or **gel**•a•tine)

ge•**la**•to

gem

gen•der

gene

ge•ne•**al**•o•gy

gen•e•ral

gen•er•al•ize

gen•er•ate

gen•er•at•ing

gen•er•**a**•tion

gen•er•**a**•tor

gen•**er**•ic

gen•er•ous

ge•**net**•ics

ge•nie

gen•ius (often confused with "genus")

Such intelligence is a mark of genius.

gen•tile

gen•tle

gen•tle•man

gen•tle•ness

gen•tle•wo•man

gent•ly

gen•tri•fi•**ca**•tion

gen•u•ine

ge•nus (often confused with "genius")

Wolves and dogs belong to the same genus.

ge•o•**de**•sic

ge•o•**graph**•i•cal

ge•**og**•ra•phy

ge•o•**log**•i•cal

ge•**ol**•o•gist

ge•**ol**•o•gy

ge•o•**met**•ric

ge•**om**•e•try

Geor•gia

ge•o•**ther**•mal

ge•**ra**•ni•um

ger•bil

ger•i•**at**•ric

germ

Ger•man

Ger•**man**•ic

Ger•man **mea**•sles

ger•mi•nate

ger•mi•nat•ing

ger•mi•**na**•tion

ges•ture

ges•tur•ing

get

get•a•way

Get•tys•burg

gey•ser

ghast•ly

ghet•to

ghost

ghost•ly

gi•ant

gib•ber•ish

gid•dy

gift

gig

gi•**gan**•tic

gig•gle

gild (sounds like "guild")

If you gild the frame, the picture will be set off quite nicely.

gill

gim•mick

gin

gin•ger

gin•ger•bread

gin•ger•ly

gin•gham

gi•**raffe**

gird•er

girl

girl•friend

girth

gist

give

gla•cier

glad

glade

glad•i•a•tor

glad•i•**o**•li (pl.)

glad•i•**o**•lus (sing.)

glad•ly

glam•or•ous

glam•our (or **glam**•or)

glance

gland

glare

glar•ing

glass

glass•es

glaze

gla•zier

glaz•ing

gleam

glee

glee•ful

glen

glide

glid•er

glid•ing

glim•mer

glimpse
glimps•ing
glint
glis•ten
glitch
glit•ter
gloat
glob•al
globe
glock•en•spiel
gloom
gloom•y
glo•ri•fi•**ca**•tion
glo•ri•fied
glo•ri•fies
glo•ri•fy
glo•ri•fy•ing
glor•i•ous
glo•ry
gloss
glos•sa•ries
glos•sa•ry
glove
glow
glow•worm
glu•cose
glue
glu•ing
glum
glut
glut•ted
glut•ting
glut•ton
gnarled

gnash
gnat
gnaw

gnaw

gnome
gnu
go
goad
goal
goal•ie
goat
goa•**tee**
gob•ble
gob•bling
gob•let
gob•lin
go-cart
God
god•dess
god•par•ent
goes
gog•gles
gold

gold•en•rod
gold•finch
gold•fish
golf
gon•do•la
gone
gong
good
good-**bye** (*or* good-**by**)
good-na•tured
good•ness
good•night
goods
good•will
goo•ey
goose
goose bumps
go•pher
gore
gorge
gor•geous
go•ril•la
gor•y
gos•pel
gos•sa•mer
gos•sip
got
Goth•ic
gouge
gourd
gour•**met** (rhymes with "say")
gov•ern
gov•ern•ment

gown
grab
grace
grace•ful
grade
grad•u•al
grad•u•ate
grad•u•at•ing
grad•u•a•tion
graf•fi•ti
graft
grain
gram
gram•mar
gram•mat•i•cal
gra•na•ries
gra•na•ry
grand
grand•child
grand•fa•ther
grand•moth•er
grand•pa•rent
grand•stand
gran•ite
gra•no•la
grant
gran•u•late
gran•u•lat•ing
gran•u•la•tion
grape
grape•fruit
grape•vine
graph

graveyard

graph•ic
graph•ics
graph•ite
grap•ple
grap•pling
grasp
grass
grass•hop•per
grass•land
grate
grate•ful
grat•i•fi•ca•tion
grat•i•fied
grat•i•fies
grat•i•fy
grat•i•tude
grave

grav•el
grave•stone
grave•yard
grav•i•ty
gra•vy
gray
graze
grease
great
Great Dane
great-grand•child
great-grand•pa•rent
greed
greed•y
green
green•horn
green•house
greet
gre•nade
grew
grey•hound
grid
grid•dle
grid•i•ron
grid•lock
grief
griev•ance
grieve
grill
grim
gri•mace
grime
grin

grind
grind·stone
grinned
grip
gris·ly (sounds like "grizzly")
Police are investigating a grisly murder.
grit
grits
griz·zly (sounds like "grisly")
A grizzly bear can be dangerous.
groan
gro·cer·ies
gro·cer·y
grog·gy
groom
groove
grope
gross
gro·tesque
grouch
grouch·y
ground
ground·ed
ground·hog
group
grove
grov·el
grow

growl
grown-up
growth
grub
grub·by
grudge
gru·el·ing
grue·some
gruff
grum·ble
grump·y
grunge
grunt
gua·ca·mo·le
guar·an·tee
guard
guard·i·an
guer·ril·la
guess
guest
gui·dance
guide
guide·book
guid·ing
guild (sounds like "gild")
There was a guild for weavers in medieval times.
guil·lo·tine
guilt
guilt·y
guin·ea pig

gui·tar
gulch
gulf
gull
gul·li·ble
gul·ly
gulp
gum
gum·drop
gun
gun·fire
gun·pow·der
gup·pies
gup·py
gur·gle
gur·gling
gush
gust
gus·to
gut
gut·ter
guy
guz·zle
gym
gym·na·si·um
gym·nast
gym·nas·tics
Gyp·sies
Gyp·sy
gy·rate
gy·rat·ing
gy·ra·tion
gy·ro·scope

ha
hab•it
hab•i•tat
ha•**bit**•u•al
ha•**bit**•u•al•ly
ha•ci•**en**•da
hack
had
had•n't
hag•gard
hag•gle
hai•ku
hail
hair (sounds like "hare")
  Please comb your hair.
hair•cut
hair•do
hair•dres•ser
hair•pin
hair-rais•ing
hair•y
half
half•heart•ed
half-**mast**
half•time
half•way
hal•i•but
hall
hal•le•**lu**•jah
hal•lowed
Hal•low•**een**
  (*or* Hal•low•**e'en**)

hal•**lu**•ci•nate
hal•**lu**•ci•nat•ing
hal•**lu**•ci•**na**•tion
hall•way
ha•lo
halt
hal•ter
halve (sounds like "have")
  To halve something is to cut it in two.
halves
ham
ham•burg•er
ham•mer
ham•mock
ham•per
ham•ster
hand
hand•bag
hand•ball
hand•book
hand•cuffs
hand•ful
hand•i•cap
hand•i•craft
hand•ker•chief
hand•ker•chiefs
  (*or* **hand**•ker•chieves)
han•dle
han•dle•bars
hand•made

hand-me-down
hand•out
hand•rail
hand•shake
hand•some
hand•spring
hand•stand
hand•writ•ing
hand•y
hang
han•gar (sounds like "hanger")
  The airplane is in the hangar.
hang•er (sounds like "hanger")
  Put the shirt on the hanger.
hang•o•ver
hang-up
han•ker
Ha•nuk•kah (*or* **Cha**•nu•kah)
hap•**haz**•ard
hap•pen
hap•pi•er
hap•pi•est
hap•pi•ness
hap•py
hap•py-go-**luck**•y

har•**ass**
also pronounced
har•ass

har•bor

hard

hard-boiled

hard•en

hard•ly

hard•ship

hard•ware

hard•wood

har•dy

hare (sounds like
"hair")

*The tortoise beat
the hare.*

harm

harm•ful

harm•less

har•**mon**•i•ca

har•mo•nize

har•mo•ny

har•ness

harp

har•**poon**

harp•si•chord

harsh

har•vest

har•vest•er

has

has•n't

has•sle

haste

has•ty

hat

hatch

hatch•back

hatch•er•y

(**hatchet**)

hatch•et

hate

hate•ful

haugh•ty

haul

haunt

have (sounds like
"halve")

I have new shoes.

ha•ven

have•n't

hav•oc

Ha•**wai**•i

hawk

hay (sounds like "hey")

Horses eat hay.

hay•loft

hay•stack

haz•ard

haz•ard•ous

haze

ha•zel

haz•y

he

head

head•ache

head•band

head•dress

head•**first**

head•ing

head•light

head•line

head•mas•ter

head•mis•tress

head-on

head•phones

head•quar•ters

head•strong

head•way

heal

health

heap

heaped

heap•ing

hear

heard (sounds like
"herd")

*I heard him say
we won.*

hear•say

hearse

heart

heart at•**tack**

heart·beat
heart·bro·ken
hearth
heart·less
heart·y
heat
heat·er
heave
heav·en
heav·en·ly
heav·y
He·brew
heck·le
hec·tic
he'd (sounds like "heed")
He'd like that.
hedge
heed (sounds like "he'd")
Heed my warning.
heel
hef·ty
heif·er
height
height·en
Heim·lich ma·**neu**·ver
heir (sounds like "air")
She is his only heir.
heir·ess
heir·loom
hel·i·cop·ter

he·li·um
hel·**lo**
hel·met
help
help·ful
help·ing
help·less
hem
hem·i·sphere
hem·lock
he·mo·**phil**·i·a
he·mo·**phil**·i·ac
hem·or·rhage
hen
her
herb
her·bi·vore
herd (sounds like "heard")
There's a herd of cows.
here
he·**red**·i·tar·y
he·**red**·i·ty

(**helicopter**)

here's
her·i·tage
her·mit
he·ro
he·roes
he·**ro**·ic
her·o·in (sounds like "heroine")
She almost died from a heroin overdose.
her·o·ine (sounds like "heroin")
The heroine saved many lives.
her·on
her·ring
hers
her·**self**
hertz (sounds like "hurts")
A hertz is a unit of measurement.
hes·i·tate
hes·i·tat·ing
hes·i·**ta**·tion
hex·a·gon
hey (sounds like "hay")
Hey, how're you?
hi (sounds like "high")
Hi, there!
hi·ber·nate
hi·ber·**na**·tion
hic·cup
hick·o·ry

hid

hide

hide-and-**seek**

hid•e•ous

hide•out

hi•er•o•**glyph**•ics

high (sounds like "hi")

The airplane is high in the sky.

higher (sounds like "hire")

Jump higher!

high•light

high-rise

high tech (n.)

high-tech (adj.)

high•way

hi•jack

hike

hi•**lar**•i•ous

hill

hill•side

hill•top

him (sounds like "hymn")

Please give him the package.

him•**self**

hind

hin•der

Hin•du•ism

hinge

hint

hip

hip-hop

hip•pie

Hip•**poc**•ra•tes

hip•po•**pot**•a•mus

hire (sounds like "higher")

I hope they hire you for the job.

Hir•o•**shi**•ma
  also pronouned
  Hi•**ro**•shi•ma

his

His•**pan**•ic

hiss

his•**tor**•ic

his•**tor**•ic•al

his•to•ries

his•to•ry

hit

hitch

hitch•hike

hit•ting

hive

hoard

hoarse (sounds like "horse")

I'm too hoarse to talk.

hoax

hob•by

hock•ey

hoe

hoes (sounds like "hose")

There are two hoes in the garden shed.

hog

ho•gan

hoist

hold

hold•up

hole (sounds like "whole")

Dig a hole and plant the seeds.

hol•i•day

ho•**lis**•tic

hol•low

hol•ly

ho•lo•caust

ho•lo•gram

hol•ster

ho•ly (sounds like "wholly")

The holy man spoke words of wisdom.

Ho•ly Com•**mun**•ion

home

home•less

home•ly

home•**made**

home•mak•er

ho•me•**op**•a•thy

home•room

home run

home•sick

home•spun

home•stead

home•work

ho•**mog**•e•nize

hom•o•graph

hom•o•nym

hom•o•phone

hon•est

hon•est•ly

hon•ey

hon•ey•bee

hon•ey•comb

hon•ey•moon

hon•ey•suck•le

honk

hon•or

hon•or•able

hon•or•ably

hon•or•ar•y

hood

hoof

hook

hooked

hoop

hoo•**ray** (or hur•**ray**)

hoot

hop

hope

hoped

hope•ful

hope•ful•ly

hope•less

hope•less•ly

Ho•pi

hop•ing

hop•scotch

ho•**ri**•zon

hor•i•**zon**•tal

hor•mone

horn

hor•net

hor•o•scope

hor•ri•ble

hor•rid

hor•**rif**•ic

hor•ri•fy

hor•ror

horse (sounds like "hoarse")

My horse loves to gallop.

horse•back

horse•fly

horse•play

horse•pow•er

horse•shoe

hose (sounds like "hoes")

Use this hose to water the garden.

ho•sier•y

hos•pice

hos•pi•tal

hos•pi•**tal**•i•ty

host

hos•tage

hos•tel (sounds like "hostile")

We stayed in a youth hostel on our trip.

host•ess

hos•tile (sounds like "hostel")

Hostile people can be frightening.

hos•**til**•i•ty

hot

hot dog

ho•**tel**

hot-wa•ter **bot**•tle

hound

hour

hour•glass

house

house•boat

house•fly

house•hold

house•work

hous•ing

hov•er

hov•er•craft

how

how•**ev**•er

howl

hub

hud•dle

hue

huff

hug

huge

hugged

hugging

hulk

hull
hum
hu•man
hu•mane
hu•man•i•**tar**•i•an
hu•**man**•i•ty
hum•ble
hum•drum
hu•mid
hu•**mil**•i•ate
hu•mil•i•**a**•tion
hu•**mil**•i•ty
hummed
hum•ming
hum•ming•bird
hu•mor
hu•mor•ous
hump
hump•back
hunch
hunch•back
hun•dred
hun•dredth
hun•gri•er
hun•gri•est
hun•gry
hunk
hunt
hunt•er
hur•dle
hurl
hur•**rah**

hur•**ray** (*or* hoo•**ray**)
hur•ri•cane
hur•ried
hur•ries
hur•ry
hur•ry•ing
hurt
hurts (sounds like
  "hertz")

*Getting a needle
sometimes hurts.*

hus•band
hush
husk
husk•y

husky

hus•tle
hus•tling
hut
hy•a•cinth
hy•brid
hy•drant
hy•dro•e•**lec**•tric
hy•dro•e•lec•**tric**•i•ty
hy•dro•foil
hy•dro•gen
hy•dro•**pon**•ics
hy•**e**•na
hy•giene
hy•**gien**•ist
hymn (sounds like
  "him")

*We sang a hymn in
church.*

hym•nal
hype
hy•per•**ac**•tive
hy•phen
hyp•no•tize
hy•po•**chon**•dri•ac
hyp•o•crite
hy•po•**der**•mic
hy•**pot**•e•nuse
hy•po•**ther**•mi•a
hy•**poth**•e•sis
hys•**ter**•i•a
hys•**ter**•i•cal

ice
ice•berg
ice•cap
ice cream
Ice•land
ice-skate (v.)
ice skate (n.)
i•ci•cle
ic•ing
i•con
i•cy
I'd
I•da•ho
i•**de**•a
i•**de**•al
i•**den**•ti•cal
i•**den**•ti•fi•**ca**•tion
i•**den**•ti•fy
id•i•om
id•i•ot
i•dle (sounds like "idol")

The idle man didn't want to work.

i•dol (sounds like "idle")

The movie star is her idol.

if
ig•loo
ig•ne•ous
ig•**nite**

ig•**ni**•tion
ig•no•rance
ig•no•rant
ig•**nore**
i•**gua**•na
ill
I'll (sounds like "aisle" and "isle")

I'll see you tomorrow.

il•**le**•gal
il•**le**•gal•ly
il•**leg**•i•ble
Il•li•**nois**
il•**lit**•er•a•cy
il•**lit**•er•ate
il•**log**•i•cal
il•**lu**•mi•nate
il•lu•mi•**na**•tion

igloo

il•**lu**•sion
il•lus•trate
il•lus•**tra**•tion
I'm
im•age
im•age•ry
i•**mag**•i•nar•y
i•**mag**•i•**na**•tion
i•**mag**•i•na•tive
im•**ag**•ine
im•i•tate
im•i•tat•ing
im•i•**ta**•tion
im•**mac**•u•late
im•ma•**ture**
im•**mea**•sur•a•ble
im•**me**•di•ate
im•**me**•di•ate•ly
im•**mense**
im•**men**•si•ty
im•**merse**
im•**mer**•sion
im•mi•grant
im•mi•**gra**•tion
im•**mo**•bi•lize
im•**mor**•al
im•**mor**•tal
im•**mune**
im•**mune sys**•tem
im•**mu**•ni•ty
im•mu•ni•**za**•tion
im•mu•nize

im•pact
im•**pair**
im•**par**•tial
im•**pa**•tient
im•**peach**
im•**peach**•ment
im•**per**•a•tive
im•**per**•fect
im•**pe**•ri•al
im•**per**•son•al
im•**per**•son•ate
im•**plant** (v.)
im•plant (n.)
im•ple•ment
im•po•**lite**
im•port (n.)
im•**port** (v.)
  also pronounced
  im•port
im•**por**•tance
im•**por**•tant
im•pos•si•**bil**•i•ty
im•**pos**•si•ble
im•**pos**•tor
im•prac•ti•cal
im•**press**
im•**pres**•sion
im•**pres**•sive
im•print (n.)
im•**print** (v.)
im•**prop**•er
im•**prove**
im•**prove**•ment
im•pro•vi•**sa**•tion

im•pro•vise
im•pu•dent
im•pulse
im•**pul**•sive
im•**pu**•ri•ty
in (sounds like"inn")
  The bird is in the nest.
in•**ac**•cu•ra•cy
in•**ac**•cu•rate
in•**ad**•e•quate
in•ap•**pro**•pri•ate
in•ar•**tic**•u•late
in•**au**•di•ble
in•**au**•gu•rate
in•au•gu•**ra**•tion
in•can•**des**•cent
in•**ca**•pa•ble
in•cense
in•**cen**•tive
in•**ces**•sant
inch
inch•worm
in•ci•dent
in•ci•**den**•tal•ly
in•**cin**•er•ate
in•**cin**•er•a•tor
in•**ci**•sion
in•cli•**na**•tion
in•**cline** (v.)
in•cline (n.)
in•**clined**
in•**clude**
in•**clu**•sion
in•co•**her**•ent

in•come
in•com•**pat**•i•ble
in•**com**•pe•tent
in•com•**plete**
in•com•pre•**hen**•si•ble
in•con•**ceiv**•a•ble
in•con•**clu**•sive
in•con•**sid**•er•ate
in•con•**spic**•u•ous
in•con•**ven**•ience
in•con•**ven**•ient
in•**cor**•por•ate
in•cor•**rect**
in•**crease** (v.)
in•crease (n.)
in•**cred**•i•ble
in•**crim**•i•nate
in•cu•bate
in•cu•ba•tor
in•**cur**•a•ble
in•**debt**•ed
in•**deed**
in•**dent**
in•de•**pen**•dence
in•de•**pen**•dent
in•de•**struc**•ti•ble
in•dex
In•di•an
In•di•**an**•a
in•di•cate
in•di•**ca**•tion
in•**dif**•fer•ent
in•di•**ges**•tion
in•**dig**•nant

in•di•go
in•di•**rect**
in•dis•**pen**•sa•ble
in•di•**vid**•u•al
in•di•vid•u•**al**•i•ty
in•di•**vis**•i•ble
in•door
in•**doors**
in•**dulge**
in•**dus**•tri•al
in•**dus**•tri•al•ize
in•dus•tries
in•dus•try
in•ef•**fi**•cien•cy
in•ef•**fi**•cient
in•e•**qual**•i•ty
in•**ert**
in•**er**•tia
in•**ev**•i•ta•ble
in•ex•**pen**•sive
in•ex•**pe**•ri•enced
in•fa•mous
in•fant
in•fan•try
in•**fat**•u•at•ed
in•**fat**•u•**a**•tion
in•**fect**
in•**fec**•tion
in•**fec**•tious
in•**fer**
in•**fer**•ence
in•**fe**•ri•or
in•**fer**•**til**•i•ty
in•**fes**•ted

in•fil•trate
in•fil•**tra**•tion
in•fi•nite
in•**fin**•i•tive
in•**fin**•i•ty
in•**firm**
in•**fir**•ma•ry
in•**flame**
in•**flam**•ma•ble
in•flam•**ma**•tion
in•**flat**•a•ble
in•**flate**
in•**fla**•tion
in•**flex**•i•ble
in•**flict**
in•flu•ence
in•flu•**en**•tial
in•flu•**en**•za
in•fo•**mer**•cial
in•**form**
in•**for**•mal
in•**for**•mal•ly
in•for•**ma**•tion
in•for•**ma**•tion•al
in•**for**•ma•tive
in•**fre**•quent
in•**fu**•ri•ate
in•**fu**•ri•at•ing
in•**gre**•di•ent
in•**ha**•bit
in•ha•**la**•tion
in•**hale**
in•**hal**•er
in•**her**•it

in•**her**•it•ance
in•**hib**•it
in•**hu**•man
in•**i**•tial
i•**ni**•ti•ate
in•i•ti•**a**•tion
in•**i**•tia•tive
in•**ject**
in•jure
in•ju•ry
in•**jus**•tice
ink
in•land
in•let
in•mate
inn (sounds like "in")
  We stayed at a
  country inn.
in•ner
in•ning
in•no•cence
in•no•cent
in•no•**va**•tion
in•**nu**•mer•ate
in•**oc**•u•late
in•pa•tient
in•put
in•**quire**
in•**quir**•y
  also pronounced
  in•quir•y
in•**quis**•i•tive
in•**sane**
in•**scribe**

in•**scrip**•tion
in•sect
in•**sec**•ti•cide
in•se•**cure**
in•**sen**•si•tive
in•sen•si•**tiv**•i•ty
in•**sert** (v.)
in•sert (n.)
in•**side**
  also pronounced
  in•side
in•sight
in•**sig**•ni•a
in•sig•**nlf**•l•cant
in•sin•**cere**
in•**sist**
in•**sis**•tence
in•**sis**•tent
in•**sol**•u•ble
in•**som**•ni•a
in•**spect**
in•**spec**•tion
in•**spec**•tor
in•**spire**
in•**stall**
in•**stall**•ment
in•stance
in•stant
in•**stead**
in•**still**
in•stinct
in•sti•tute
in•sti•**tu**•tion
in•sti•**tu**•tion•al

in•**struct**
in•**struc**•tion
in•stru•ment

instrument

in•suf•**fi**•cient
in•su•late
in•su•lin
in•**sult** (v.)
in•sult (n.)
in•**sur**•ance
in•**sure**
in•te•ger
in•te•grate
in•te•**gra**•tion
in•**teg**•rity
in•tel•lect
in•tel•**lec**•tu•al
in•**tel**•li•gence
in•**tel**•li•gent
in•**tel**•li•gi•ble
in•**tend**
in•**tense**

in•**ten**•si•fy
in•**tent**
in•**ten**•tion
in•ter•**ac**•tive
in•ter•**cept**
in•ter•**change**•a•ble
in•ter•com
in•ter•est
in•ter•face
in•ter•**fere**
in•ter•**fer**•ence
in•ter•ga•**lac**•tic
in•**te**•ri•or
in•ter•**jec**•tion
in•ter•**me**•di•ate
in•ter•**mis**•sion
in•ter•**mit**•lent
in•tern
in•**ter**•nal
in•ter•**na**•tion•al
In•ter•net
in•ter•**plan**•e•tar•y
in•**ter**•pret
in•ter•pre•**ta**•tion
in•**ter**•ro•gate
in•ter•**rupt**
in•ter•**sect**
in•ter•**sec**•tion
  also pronounced
  in•ter•sec•tion
in•ter•**state**
in•ter•val
in•ter•**vene**
in•ter•view

in•**tes**•tine
in•ti•mate
in•**tim**•i•date
in•tim•i•**da**•tion
in•to
in•**tol**•er•a•ble
in•**tol**•er•ance
in•**tol**•er•ant
in•**tox**•i•ca•ted
in•**tran**•si•tive
in•tri•cate
in•trigue
in•tro•**duce**
in•tro•**duc**•tion
in•tro•**duc**•to•ry
in•tro•vert
in•**trude**
in•tu•**i**•tion
In•u•it
in•**vade**
in•va•lid (n.)
in•**val**•id (adj.)
in•**val**•u•a•ble
in•**var**•i•a•bly
in•**vent**
in•**ven**•tion
in•ven•to•ry
in•**vert**
in•**ver**•te•brate
in•**vest**
in•**ves**•ti•gate

in•**vin**•ci•ble
in•**vis**•i•ble
in•vi•**ta**•tion
in•**vite**
in•**volve**
in•**volved**
in•ward
i•o•dine
i•on
I•o•wa
i•rate
also pronounced
i•**rate**
i•ris
I•rish
i•ron
i•**ron**•ic
i•ro•ny
I•ro•quois
ir•**ra**•tio•nal
ir•**reg**•u•lar
ir•**rel**•e•vance
ir•**rel**•e•vant
ir•re•**sist**•i•ble
ir•re•**spon**•si•ble
ir•re•**vers**•i•ble
ir•ri•gate
ir•ri•**ga**•tion
ir•ri•ta•ble
ir•ri•tate
ir•ri•**ta**•tion

Is•lam
Is•lam•ic
is•land
isle (sounds like "aisle"
  and "I'll")
  We went to a small,
  sunny isle for our
  vacation.
is•n't
i•so•late
i•so•**met**•rics
i•**sos**•ce•les
is•sue
isth•mus
it
i•**tal**•ic
itch
i•tem
i•tem•ize
i•**tin**•er•ar•y
its (sounds like "it's")
  The dog buried its
  bone.
it's (sounds like "its")
  It's time to go.
it•**self**
I've
i•vo•ry
i•vy

jab
jabbed
jab•bing
jack
jack•et
jack•ham•mer
jack•knife
jack-o'-lan•tern
jack•pot
jack•rab•bit
Ja•**cuz**•zi
jade
jag•ged
jag•uar
jail
jail•bird
jam
jam•bor•**ee**
jan•i•tor
Jan•u•ar•y
Ja•**pan**
Jap•a•**nese**
jar
jar•gon
jave•lin
jaw
jay•walk
jazz
jeal•ous
jeans
jeep
jeer

Je•**ho**•vah
Jell-O
jel•ly
jel•ly•fish
jeop•ar•dize
jeop•ard•y
jerk
jest
jest•er

jester

Je•sus
jet
jet•ti•son
jet•ty
Jew
jew•el

jew•el•er
jew•el•ry
Jew•ish
jif•fy
jig
jig•saw
jin•gle
jinx
job
jock•ey
jog
jogged
jog•ger
jog•ging
join
join•er
joint
joke
jol•ly
jolt
jon•quil
jour•nal
jour•na•lism
jour•nal•ist
jour•ney
joust
jo•vi•al
jowl
joy
joy•ful
joy•ous
joy•stick

ju•bi•lant
ju•bi•**la•**tion
ju•bi•lee
Ju•da•ism
judge
judg•ment (*or*
  judge•ment)
ju•**di•**cial
ju•**di•**cious
ju•do
jug
jug•gle

juice
juke•box
Ju•**ly**
jum•ble
jum•bo
jump
jum•per
junc•tion
June
jun•gle
jun•ior
junk

junk•yard
Ju•pi•ter
ju•ror
ju•ry
just
jus•tice
jus•ti•fi•**ca•**tion
jus•ti•fied
jus•ti•fies
jus•ti•fy
ju•ve•nile
jux•ta•**pose**

ka•**bob** (or ke•**bob**)

ka•**lei**•do•scope

kan•ga•**roo**

Kan•sas

kar•a•**o**•ke

kar•at (sounds like "carat," "caret," and "carrot")

This bracelet is made of 14-karat gold.

ka•**ra**•te

kay•ak

ke•**bob** (or ka•**bob**)

keen

keep

keep•er

keep•sake

kelp

ken•nel

Ken•**tuck**•y

kept

ker•chief

ker•chiefs (or **ker**•chieves)

ker•nel

ker•o•sene

ketch•up

ket•tle

ket•tle•drum

key (sounds like "quay")

Here is the key to the door.

key•board

key•hole

key•pad

kha•ki

kib•**butz**

kick

kitten

kick•off

kid

kid•ded

kid•ding

kid•nap

kid•nap•per

kid•nap•ping

kid•ney

kill

kiln

ki•lo•gram

ki•**lo**•meter

ki•lo•watt

kilt

ki•**mo**•no

kin

kind

kin•der•gar•ten

kind•heart•ed

kind•ness

ki•**net**•ic

king

king•dom

kink

kin•ship

ki•osk

kiss

kit

kitch•en

kite

kit•ten

kit•ty

ki•wi

klep•to•**ma**•ni•ac

klutz

knack

knap•sack

knave

knead (sounds like "need")

Please knead the dough.

knee

kneel

knew

knick•ers

knife

knight (sounds like "night")

A knight slew the dragon.

knight·hood

knit (sounds like "nit")

I'll knit a sweater for Grandma.

knit·ted

knit·ting

knives

knob

knock

knock·er

knoll

knot (sounds like "not")

He tied a square knot.

knot·ty

know (sounds like "no")

I know the name of the secret guest.

know-how

know·ledge

known

knuck·le

ko·**a**·la

kook

Ko·**ran** (*or* Qur'·**an**)

Ko·**re**·a

kos·her

Krem·lin

kryp·ton

kum·quat

kung fu

Kwan·za (*or* **Kwan**·zaa)

lab
la·bel
la·beled
la·bor
lab·o·ra·tor·ies
lab·o·ra·tor·y
lace
lac·ing
lack
lacks (sounds like
  "lax")
  This sauce lacks
  flavor.
lack·a·**dai**·si·cal
lack·lus·ter
lac·quer
la·**crosse**
lad
lad·der

(ladder)

la·dies
la·dle
la·dy
la·dy·bug
lag
lagged
lag·ging
la·**goon**
laid-back
lake
lamb
lame
lamp
lance
lanc·ing
land
land·fill
land·ing
land·la·dies
land·la·dy
land·lord
land·mark
land·scape
land·slide
lane
lan·guage
lank·y
lan·tern
lan·yard
lap
la·**pel**
Lap·land

lap·top
lard
large
large·ly
la·ri·at
lark
lar·va (sing.)
lar·vae (pl.)
lar·yn·**gi**·tis
lar·ynx
la·**sa**·gna (*or*
  la·**sa**·gne)
la·ser
lash
lass
las·so
  also pronounced
  las·**so**
las·sos (*or* las·soes)
last
last·ing
latch
latch·key
late
late·com·er
late·ly
lat·er·al
la·tex
lathe
lath·er
Lat·in
La·**ti**·na

Lat•in
  A•**mer**•i•can
La•**ti**•no
lat•i•tude
laugh
laugh•a•ble
laugh•ter
launch
laun•der
laun•dries
laun•dry
lau•rel
la•va
lav•a•tory
lav•en•der
lav•ish
law
law-a•**bid**•ing
law•ful
lawn
lawn•mow•er
law•suit
law•yer
lax (sounds like
  "lacks")
  The teacher was lax in
  collecting homework.
lay (sounds like "lei")
  Did the hen lay
  this egg?
lay•er
lay•off
lay•out
la•zi•er

la•zi•est
la•zi•ness
la•zy
lead (rhymes with
  "bead")
  The guide will lead
  us out of the
  jungle.
lead (rhymes with
  "bed")
  Lead is a heavy
  metal.
lead•er•**ship**
leaf
leaf•let
league
leak (sounds like
  "leek")
  The plumber fixed
  the leak.

lawnmower

lean
lean•ing
leap
leap•frog

learn
learned
learn•ing
lease
leash
least
leath•er
leave
leaves
leav•ing
Leb•a•non
lec•ture
ledge
leech
leek (sounds like
  "leak")
  A leek is related to
  an onion.
left
left-hand•ed
left•overs
leg
leg•a•cies
leg•a•cy
le•gal
leg•end
leg•gings
leg•i•ble
le•gion
leg•is•late
leg•is•**la**•tion
leg•is•la•tor
leg•is•la•ture
le•**git**•i•mate

lei (sounds like "lay")

The girl wore a lei of orchids around her neck.

leis•ure

lei•sure•ly

lem•on

lem•on•ade

lend

length

length•en

le•ni•ent

lens

lens•es

Lent

len•til

leop•ard

le•o•tard

less

les•sen (sounds like "lesson")

This medicine will lessen the pain.

less•ened

les•son (sounds like "lessen")

The math lesson wasn't so hard.

let

leth•al

let's

let•ter

let•ter•ing

let•ting

let•tuce

leu•ke•mi•a

lev•ee (sounds like "levy")

The levee holds the river back.

lev•el

lev•er

lev•i•tate

lev•y (sounds like "levee")

The council will levy a new tax.

li•a•ble

li•ar (sounds like "lyre")

She has a reputation as a liar.

lib•er•al

lib•er•al•ism

lib•er•ate

lib•er•at•ed

lib•er•at•ing

lib•er•a•tion

Li•be•ria

lib•er•ties

lib•er•ty

li•brar•i•an

li•brar•ies

li•brar•y

lice

li•cense

li•cens•ing

lick

lic•o•rice

lid

lie (sounds like "lye")

Lie back and relax.

lieu•ten•ant

life

life•boat

life•guard

life•less

life•like

life•long

life pre•serv•er

life•style

life•time

lift

lift•off

lig•a•ment

light

light•en

light•house

light•ning

light•weight

light-year

lik•a•ble

like

like•ly

like•ness

li•lac

lil•ies

lil•y

limb

lim•ber

lime

lime•light

lim•er•ick
lime•stone
lim•it
lim•it•ed
lim•it•less
limp
Lin•coln
line
lin•e•ar
lin•en
lin•ger
lin•**gui**•ne
lin•ing
link
li•**no**•le•um
lint
li•on
li•on•ess
lip
lip-read
lip•stick
liq•ue•fy
liq•uid
liq•uor
lisp
list
lis•ten
li•ter
lit•er•a•cy
lit•er•al•ly
lit•er•ate
lit•er•a•ture
lit•mus pa•per
lit•ter

lit•tle
liv•a•ble
live
live•li•hood
live•ly
liv•er
live•stock
liv•id
liv•ing
liz•ard
lla•ma
load
loaf
loaf•er
loam
loan (sounds like
"lone")
*I need a loan from
the bank.*
loathe
loath•some
loaves
lob
lobbed
lob•bies
lob•bing
lob•by
lob•ster
lo•cal
lo•cal•ly
lo•cate
lo•cat•ed
lo•cat•ing
lo•**ca**•tion

lock
lock•er
lock•er **room**
lock•et
lock•jaw
lock•smith
lo•co•**mo**•tion
lo•co•**mo**•tive
lodge
lodg•er
loft
loft•y
log
logged
log•ging
log•ic
lo•go
loin
loi•ter
loll
lol•li•pop
lone (sounds like
"loan")
*She was the lone
person on the bus.*
lone•li•ness
lone•ly
lone•some
long
long-dis•tance
long•hand
lon•gi•tude
long-range
long•ship

long-term
long-**win**•ded
loo•fah
look
look•ing
look•out
loon
loop
loose
loose-leaf
loos•en
loot (sounds like "lute")

The loot was hidden underneath a floorboard.

lop•sid•ed
lord
lose
lo•sing
loss
lot
lo•tion
lot•ter•ies
lot•ter•y
lo•tus
loud
loud•speak•er
Lou•i•si•**an**•a
lounge
lov•a•ble
love
love•bird
love•li•est

love•ly
low
low•er
low•er•**case**
loy•al
loy•al•ly
loy•al•ty
lu•bri•cate
luck
luck•i•ly
luck•y
lu•di•crous
lug
lug•gage
lugged

(**luggage**)

lug•ging
luke•warm
lull
lul•la•by

lum•ber
lum•ber•jack
lu•mi•nous
lump
lump•y
lu•nar
lunch
lung
lunge
lurch
lure
lur•ing
lurk
lus•cious
lush
lust
lus•ter
lute (sounds like "loot")

The lute is a musical instrument.

lux•u•ries
lux•u•ry
lye (sounds like "lie")

Be careful when you pour the lye.

Lyme dis•**ease**
lymph
lynx
lyre (sounds like "liar")

She played the lyre while he sang.

lyr•ic
lyr•i•cal
lyr•ics

ma'am
ma•**ca**•bre
mac•a•**ro**•ni
ma•**chet**•e
ma•**chine**
ma•**chin**•er•y
ma•**chin**•ist
mack•er•el
mad
mad•am
mag•a•zine
mag•ic
mag•i•cal
mag•i•cal•ly
ma•**gi**•cian
mag•ma
mag•**ne**•si•um
mag•net
mag•**net**•ic
mag•net•ize
mag•ni•fi•**ca**•tion
mag•**nif**•i•cence
mag•**nif**•i•cent
mag•ni•fied
mag•ni•fi•er
mag•ni•fies
mag•ni•fy
mag•ni•tude
mag•**no**•li•a
ma•**hog**•a•ny
maid
maid•en

mail (sounds like "male")
The check is in the mail.
mail•box
mail car•ri•er

mail carrier

mail•man
maim
main (sounds like "Maine" and "mane")
I don't understand the main idea.
Maine (sounds like "main" and "mane")
Delicious lobsters come from Maine.
main•frame
main•land

main•ly
main•stay
main•stream
main•**tain**
maize (sounds like "maze")
Maize is another word for corn.
ma•jes•tic
ma•**jes**•ti•cal•ly
maj•es•ties
maj•es•ty
ma•jor
ma•jor•**ette**
ma•**jor**•i•ty
make
make-be•lieve
make•shift
make•up
ma•**lar**•i•a
male (sounds like "mail")
That male bird has bright feathers.
mal•ice
ma•**li**•cious
ma•**lig**•nan•cies
ma•**lig**•nan•cy
ma•**lig**•nant
mall
mal•lard
mal•let

mal•nu•**tri**•tion

malt

malt•ed

mam•mal

mam•moth

man

man•age

man•a•ger

man•a-tee

Man•da•rin

man•date

man•do•lin

mane (sounds like "Maine" and "main")

Be sure to brush the horse's mane.

ma•**neu**•ver

man•ger

man•gle

man•go

Man•**hat**•tan

man•hole

man•hood

ma•ni•ac

man•i•cure

ma•**nip**•u•late

ma•nip•u•**la**•tion

man•kind

man-made

manned

man•ner (sounds like "manor")

They spoke in a friendly manner.

man•ning

man•or (sounds like "manner")

The duke was the lord of the manor.

man•sion

man•slaugh•ter

man•u•al

man•u•**fac**•ture

man•u•**fac**•tur•er

man•u•**fac**•tur•ing

ma•**nure**

man•u•script

man•y

map

ma•ple

mar•a•thon

mar•ble

march

March

Mar•di Gras

mare

mar•ga•rine

mar•gin

mar•i•gold

mar•i•**juan**•a

ma•**ri**•na

mar•i•**na**•ra

ma•**rine**

Ma•**rine Corps**

mar•i•o•**nette**

mar•i•time

mark

mar•ket

mar•ma•lade

ma•**roon**

ma•**rooned**

ma•**roon**•ing

mar•**quee**

mar•riage

mar•ried

mar•ries

mar•row

mar•ry

mar•ry•ing

Mars

marsh

mar•shal (sounds like "martial")

The marshal arrested the cow thief.

marsh•mal•low

mar•**su**•pi•al

mar•tial (sounds like "marshal")

During the war, martial law was declared.

Mar•tin **Lu**•ther **King,** Jr.

mar•tyr

mar•tyr•dom

mar•vel

mar•vel•ous

mar•vel•ous•ly

Mar•y•land

mas•**car**•a

mas•cot

mas•cu•line

mash
mask
ma•son
ma•son•ry
mas•quer•ade
mass
Mas•sa•chu•setts
mas•sa•cre
mas•sage
mas•sive
mass me•di•a
mass tran•sit
mast
mas•ter
mas•ter•mind
mas•ter•piece
mat
mat•a•dor
match
mate
ma•te•ri•al
ma•te•ri•al•is•tic
ma•te•ri•al•ize
ma•ter•nal
ma•ter•ni•ty
math
math•e•mat•i•cal
math•e•ma•ti•cian
math•e•mat•ics
mat•i•nee
mat•ri•mo•ny
ma•tron
matte
mat•ted

mat•ter
mat•tress
ma•ture
ma•ture•ly
ma•tu•ri•ty
maul
mau•so•le•um
mauve
max•i•mum
may
May
Ma•ya
Ma•yan
may•be
May•day
may•hem
May•flow•er
may•on•naise
  also pronounced
  may•on•naise
may•or
maze (sounds
  like"maize")
  I got lost in the maze.
me
mead•ow
mea•ger
meal
mean
me•an•der
mean•ing
meant
mean•time
mean•while

mea•sles
mea•sly
meas•ure
meat (sounds like
  "meet")
  *She's a meat-and-
  potatoes kid.*
me•chan•ic
me•chan•i•cal
mech•a•nism
med•al (sounds like
  "meddle")
  *She won a medal
  for bravery.*
med•dle (sounds like
  "medal")
  *Don't meddle in their
  friendship.*
med•dle•some
med•dling
me•di•a
me•di•an
med•ic
Med•i•caid
med•i•cal
med•i•cal•ly
Med•i•care
med•i•cine
me•di•e•val
me•di•o•cre
med•i•tate
med•i•tat•ed
med•i•tat•ing
med•i•ta•tion

me•di•um
med•ley
meek
meet (sounds like
  "meat")
  *I'd like you to meet
  my mom.*
meet•ing
meg•a•byte
meg•a•phone
mel•an•**chol**•ic
mel•an•cho•ly
meld
mel•low
me•**lod**•ic
mel•o•dies
me•**lo**•di•ous
me•**lo**•di•ous•ness
mel•o•dra•ma
mel•o•dra•**mat**•ic
mel•o•dy
mel•on
melt
melt•down
mem•ber
mem•ber•ship
mem•brane
me•**men**•to
mem•o
mem•oir
mem•o•ra•**bil**•ia
mem•o•ra•ble
mem•o•**ran**•dum
me•**mo**•ri•al

mem•o•ries
mem•o•rize
mem•o•riz•ing
mem•o•ry
men
men•ace
mend
me•**no**•rah

menorah

men•tal
men•tion
men•u
me•**ow**
mer•ce•nar•ies
mer•ce•nar•y
mer•chan•dise
mer•chant
mer•cies
merc•i•ful
mer•cu•ry
Mer•cu•ry

mer•cy
mere
mere•ly
merge
merg•er
me•**rid**•i•an
mer•it
mer•maid
mer•ri•er
mer•ri•est
mer•ri•ness
mer•ry
mer•ry-go-round
me•sa
mesh
mess
mes•sage
mes•sen•ger
me•**tab**•o•lism
met•al
met•a•**mor**•pho•sis
met•a•phor
me•te•or
me•te•or•ite
me•te•o•**rol**•o•gist
me•te•or•**ol**•o•gy
me•ter
meth•ane
meth•od
me•**thod**•i•cal
me•**tic**•u•lous
met•ric
met•ro•**pol**•i•tan
mice

Mich•i•gan
mi•crobe
mi•cro•chip
mi•cro•com•pu•ter
mi•cro•**or**•gan•ism
mi•cro•phone
mi•cro•scope
mi•cro•**scop**•ic
mi•cro•wave
mid•day
mid•dle
mid•dle-**aged**
Mid•dle **Ag**•es
Mid•dle **East**
mid•get
mid•night
mid•way
Mid•**west**
mid•wife
might
mi•graine
mi•grant
mi•grate
mi•grat•ing
mi•**gra**•tion
mi•gra•to•ry
mild
mil•dew
mile
mile•stone
mil•i•tant
mil•i•tar•y
mi•**li**•tia
milk

milk•y
Milk•y **Way**
mill
mil•**len**•ni•um
mil•li•gram
mil•li•me•ter
mil•lion
mil•lion•**aire**
mime
mim•ic
mince
mince•meat
mind
mine
min•er (sounds like
    "minor")

*The men all worked
as coal miners.*

(**miner**)

min•e•ral
min•gle

min•i•a•ture
min•i•mize
min•i•mum
min•i•ser•ies
min•i•skirt
min•is•ter
min•is•tered
mink
Min•ne•**so**•ta
min•now
mi•nor (sounds like
    "miner")

*Since he's a minor, he
needs his parents'
permission.*

mi•**nor**•i•ty
min•strel
mint
min•u•end
mi•nus
min•ute (n.)
min•**ute** (adj.)
min•ute•man
mir•a•cle
mi•**rage**
mir•ror
mis•be•**have**
mis•be•**hav**•ing
mis•be•**hav**•ior
mis•**cal**•cu•late
mis•cal•cu•**la**•tion
mis•**car**•riage
  also pronounced
  mis•car•riage

mis•cel•**la**•ne•ous
mis•chief
mis•**con**•duct
mi•ser
mis•er•a•ble
mis•fit
mis•**for**•tune
mis•**giv**•ing
mis•**guid**•ed
mis•hap
mis•in•**form**
mis•in•for•**ma**•tion
mis•**lay**
mis•**lead**
mis•**place**
mis•print
mis•pro•**nounce**
miss
mis•sile
mis•sing
mis•sion
mis•sion•ar•y
Mis•sis•**sip**•pi
Mis•**sou**•ri
mis•**spell**
mist
mis•**take**
mis•**tak**•en
mis•**tak**•en•ly
mis•ter
mis•tle•toe
mis•**took**
mis•**treat**
mis•**treat**•ment

mis•tress
mis•**trust**
mis•un•der•**stand**
mis•un•der•**stand**•ing
mis•un•der•**stood**
mis•**use**
mite
mitt
mit•ten
mix
mix•ture
mix-up
moan
moat
mob
mobbed
mob•bing
mo•bile
moc•ca•sin
mock
mock•ing•bird
mode
mod•el
mo•dem
mod•er•ate
mod•er•at•ing
mod•er•**a**•tion
mod•ern
mod•ern•i•**za**•tion
mod•ern•ize
mod•est
mod•es•ty
mod•i•fi•**ca**•tion
mod•i•fied

mod•i•fi•er
mod•i•fies
mod•i•fy
mod•ule
Mo•**ham**•med
  (*or* Mu•**ham**•mad)
Mo•hawk
moist
moist•en
moist•ure
mo•lar
mo•**las**•ses
mold
mold•y
mole
mo•**lec**•u•lar
mol•e•cule
mol•lusk
molt
mol•ten
mom
mo•ment
mo•men•**tar**•i•ly
mo•men•tar•y
mo•**men**•tum
mon•arch
mon•ar•chy
mon•as•ter•ies
mon•as•ter•y
mo•**nas**•tic
Mon•day
mon•ey
Mon•**go**•li•a
mon•i•tor

monk
mon•key
mon•key **wrench**
mon•o•**lin**•gual
mon•o•logue
mon•o•nu•cle•**o**•sis
mo•**nop**•o•lies
mo•nop•o•**lis**•tic
mo•**nop**•o•lize
mo•**nop**•o•liz•ing
mo•**nop**•o•ly
mon•o•rail
mo•**not**•o•nous
mo•**not**•o•ny
mon•**soon**
mon•ster
mon•**stros**•i•ty
mon•strous
Mon•**tan**•a
Mon•te•**zu**•ma
month
month•ly
mon•u•ment
mon•u•**men**•tal
mon•u•**men**•tal•ly
mood
mood•y
moon
moon•light
moor (sounds like
   "more")
   *Moor your boat to
   the dock.*
moose (sounds like

"mousse")
*We saw a moose in
the woods.*
mop
mope
moped
mopped
mop•ping
mor•al
mo•**rale**
mo•**ral**•i•ty
mor•al•ly
mor•bid
more (sounds like
   "moor")
   I want more, not less.
more•**o**•ver
Mor•mon
morn•ing (sounds like
   "mourning")
   *Every morning I
   watch the sunrise.*
morn•ing **glo**•ry
mo•**rose**
morph
Morse code
mor•sel
mor•tal
mor•**tal**•i•ty
mor•tar
mort•gage
mor•tu•ar•y
mo•**sa**•ic
Mos•cow

Mo•ses
mosh•ing
Mos•lem (*or* **Mus**•lim)
mosque
mos•**qui**•to
moss
most
most•ly
mo•tel
moth
moth•er
moth•er-in-law
moth•ers-in-law
Moth•er's **Day**
mo•tion
mo•tion•less
mo•ti•vate
mo•ti•vat•ing
mo•ti•**va**•tion
mo•tive
mo•tor
mo•tor•bike
mo•tor•boat
mo•tor•cade
mo•tor•cy•cle
mo•tor•ist
mot•tled
mot•to
mound
mount
moun•tain
moun•tain•**eer**
mourn
mourn•er

mourn•ful

mourn•ing (sounds like "morning")

They are mourning his death.

mouse

mousse (sounds like "moose")

Chocolate mousse is a great dessert.

mous•tache (or mus•tache)

moustache

mous•y

mouth

mouth•piece

mov•a•ble (or move•a•ble)

move

move•ment

mov•ie

mov•ing

mow

moz•za•rel•la

Mr.

Mrs.

Ms.

much

muck

mu•cus

mud

mud•di•er

mud•di•est

mud•dle

mud•dy

mud•guard

muf•fin

muf•fle

muf•fler

mug

mug•gy

Mu•ham•mad (or Mo•ham•med)

mul•ber•ry

mule

mul•ti•cul•tur•al

mul•ti•lin•gual

mul•ti•me•di•a

mul•ti•na•tion•al

mul•ti•ple

mul•ti•ple scle•ro•sis

mul•ti•pli•cand

mul•ti•pli•ca•tion

mul•ti•plied

mul•ti•pli•er

mul•ti•plies

mul•ti•ply

mul•ti•ply•ing

mul•ti•ra•cial

mul•ti•tude

mum•ble

mum•mies

mum•my

mumps

munch

mun•dane

mu•nic•i•pal

mu•nic•i•pal•i•ty

mu•ral

mur•der

murk•i•er

murk•i•est

murk•i•ness

murk•y

mur•mur

mus•cle (sounds like "mussel")

This muscle is sore.

mus•cu•lar

muse

mu•se•um

mush

mush•room

mu•sic

mu•si•cal

mu•si•cian

musk

mus•ket

mus•ket•eer

musk•rat

Mus•lim (*or* **Mos**•lem)

mus•sel (sounds
  like "muscle")

*The shell of this
steamed mussel
didn't open.*

must

mus•tache (*or*
  mous•tache)

mus•tang

mus•tard

must•n't

must•y

mu•tant

mu•tate

mu•**ta**•tion

mute

mu•ti•late

mu•ti•**la**•tion

mu•ti•nies

mu•ti•nous

mu•ti•ny

mutt

mut•ter

mut•ton

mu•tu•al

muz•zle

muz•zling

my

my•nah (*or* **my**•na)

my•ri•ad

my•**self**

mys•ter•ies

mys•**te**•ri•ous

mys•ter•y

mys•ti•fy

myth

myth•i•cal

myth•o•**log**•i•cal

my•**thol**•o•gies

my•**thol**•o•gy

nab
nabbed
nab•bing
nag
Na•ga•**sa**•ki
nagged
nag•ging
nail
na•**ive**
na•ked
na•ked•ness
name
nam•ing
nan•nies
nan•ny
nap
nap•kin
nar•**cis**•sus
nar•**cot**•ic
nar•rate
nar•ra•tive
nar•row
na•sal
nas•ti•er
nas•ti•est
nas•ti•ness
nas•**tur**•tium
nas•ty
na•tion
na•tion•al
na•tion•al•ism
na•tion•al•ist

na•tion•al•**is**•tic
na•tion•**al**•i•ties
na•tion•**al**•i•ty
na•tion•al•ize
na•tion•al•iz•ing
na•tive
Na•tive A•**mer**•i•can
Na•**tiv**•i•ty
nat•u•ral
nat•u•ral•ist
nat•u•ral•ize
nat•u•ral•ly
na•ture
naugh•ti•er
naught•i•est
naugh•ti•ness
naught•y
nau•se•a

narcissus

nau•se•ate
nau•se•at•ing
nau•seous
nau•ti•cal
Na•va•jo (*or* **Na**•va•ho)
na•val (sounds like "navel")
England was a great naval power.
na•vel (sounds like "naval")
Your navel is your belly button.
nav•i•ga•ble
nav•i•gate
nav•i•gat•ing
nav•i•**ga**•tion
nav•i•ga•tor
na•vy
Na•zi
Na•zi•sm
Ne•**an**•der•thal
near
near•by
near•ly
near•**sight**•ed
neat
neat•ness
Ne•**bras**•ka
neb•u•la (sing.)
neb•u•lae (pl.)
neb•u•las (pl.)

neb•u•lous

nec•es•**sar**•i•ly

nec•es•sar•y

ne•**ces**•si•tate

ne•**ces**•si•ties

ne•**ces**•si•ty

neck

neck•er•chief

neck•lace

neck•tie

nec•tar

need (sounds like "knead")

I need a nickel.

need•ed

need•i•er

need•i•est

nee•dle

need•less

need•less•ly

nee•dle•work

need•n't

need•y

neg•a•tive

neg•**lect**

neg•**lect**•ful

neg•li•gence

neg•li•gent

ne•**go**•tia•ble

ne•**go**•ti•ate

ne•**go**•ti•at•ing

ne•go•ti•**a**•tion

ne•**go**•ti•a•tor

neigh

neigh•bor

neigh•bor•hood

neigh•bor•ly

nei•ther

newborn

ne•on

neph•ew

Nep•tune

nerd

nerve

nerv•ous

nest

nes•tle

nes•tling

net

net•ted

net•ting

net•work

neu•ter

neu•tral

neu•**tral**•i•ty

neu•tra•lize

neu•tron

Ne•**vad**•a

nev•er

nev•er•**more**

nev•er•the•**less**

new

new•born

new•com•er

New **Eng**•land

New•found•land

New Hamp•shire

New Jer•sey

New Mex•i•co

news

news•cast

news•cast•er

news•let•ter

news•pa•per

news•print

news•stand

newt

New Tes•ta•ment

New York

New Zea•land

next

Ni•**ag**•a•ra

nib•ble

nib•bling

Nic•a•**ra**•gua

nice

nic•er

nic•est

niche

nick

nick•el

nick•name

nic•o•tine

niece

night (sounds like "knight")

Last night it was very warm.

night•fall

night•gown

night•in•gale

night•ly

night•mare

nim•ble

nine

nine•ty

nin•ja

ninth

nip

nipped

nip•ple

nit (sounds like "knit")

Please pick the nit out of my hair.

ni•tro•gen

no (sounds like "know")

No, thank you.

no•bil•i•ty

no•ble

no•ble•man

no•ble•ness

no•blesse o•blige

no•ble•wom•an

no•bly

no•bod•ies

no•bod•y

noc•tur•nal

nod

nod•ded

nod•ding

noise

nois•y

no•mad

no•mad•ic

nom•i•nate

nom•i•nat•ing

nom•i•na•tion

nom•i•nee

non•com•mit•tal

none•the•less

non•fic•tion

non•sense

non•stop

noo•dle

noon

no one

noose

nor

nor•mal

nor•mal•cy

nor•mal•i•ty

north

North A•mer•i•ca

North Car•o•li•na

North Da•ko•ta

North•east

North•ern Hem•i•sphere

North•west

Nor•way

Nor•we•gian

nose

nos•tal•gia

nos•tal•gic

nos•tril

nos•y

not (sounds like "knot")

I will not do that!

no•ta•ble

no•ta•bly

no•ta•tion

notch

note

note•book

noth•ing

no•tice

no•tice•able

no•tice•a•bly

no•ticed

no•tic•ing

no•ti•fi•ca•tion

no•ti•fied

no•ti•fies

no•ti•fy

no•tion

no•to•ri•e•ty

no•to•ri•ous

noun
nour•ish
nour•ish•ment
nov•el
nov•el•ties
nov•el•ty
No•**vem**•ber
nov•ice
no•vo•caine
now
no•where
noz•zle
nu•cle•ar
nu•cle•us
nude
nudge

nudg•ing
nud•ist
nug•get
nui•sance
numb
num•ber
nu•mer•al
nu•mer•a•tor
nu•**mer**•i•cal
nu•mer•ous
nun
nup•tial
nurse
nurs•er•ies
nurs•er•y
nurs•ing

nur•ture
nur•tur•ing
nut
nut•crack•er
nut•meg
nu•tri•ent
nu•**tri**•tion
nu•**tri**•tious
nut•shell
nut•tier
nut•tiest
nut•ti•ness
nuz•zle
nuz•zling
ny•lon
nymph

oak

oar

oar•lock

o•**a**•ses (pl.)

o•**a**•sis (sing.)

oat

oath

oat•meal

o•**be**•di•ence

o•**be**•di•ent

ob•**ese**

o•**bes**•i•ty

o•**bey**

o•**bit**•u•ar•ies

o•**bit**•u•ar•y

ob•**ject** (v.)

ob•ject (n.)

ob•**jec**•tion

ob•**jec**•tive

ob•li•gate

ob•li•**ga**•tion

o•**blige**

o•**blig**•ing

ob•**liv**•i•on

ob•**liv**•i•ous

ob•long

ob•**nox**•ious

o•boe

o•bo•ist

ob•**scene**

ob•**scen**•i•ties

ob•**scen**•i•ty

ob•**scure**

ob•**serv**•ance

ob•**serv**•ant

ob•ser•**va**•tion

ob•**serv**•a•to•ries

ob•**serv**•a•to•ry

ob•**serve**

ob•**serv**•ing

ob•**sess**

ob•**ses**•sion

ob•**ses**•sive

ob•so•lete

  also pronounced
  ob•so•**lete**

ob•sta•cle

ob•ste•**tri**•cian

ob•sti•nate

ob•**struct**

oboist

ob•**struc**•tion

ob•**tain**

ob•**tuse**

ob•vi•ous

oc•**ca**•sion

oc•**ca**•sio•nal

oc•cu•pan•cy

oc•cu•pant

oc•cu•**pa**•tion

oc•cu•**pa**•tion•al

oc•cu•pi•er

oc•cu•py

oc•**cur**

oc•**curred**

oc•**cur**•rence

oc•**cur**•ring

o•cean

o•ce•**an**•ic

o•cean•**og**•ra•pher

o•cean•**og**•ra•phy

oce•lot

o'**clock**

oc•ta•gon

oc•**tag**•o•nal

oc•ta•**he**•dron

oc•tave

Oc•**to**•ber

oc•to•ge•**nar**•i•an

oc•to•pus

odd

odd•i•ty

odds

O

ode (sounds like "owed")

My poem is an ode to nature.

o•di•ous

o•dor

Od•ys•sey

of

off

of•**fend**

of•**fend**•er

of•**fense**

of•**fen**•sive

of•fer

of•fer•ing

off•hand

of•fice

of•fi•cer

of•**fi**•cial

off-peak

off•**side**

off•spring

off-the-wall

of•ten

o•gre

oh

O•hi•o

ohm

oil

oint•ment

O•**jib**•wa

o•**kay** (*or* **OK**)

o•kayed

Ok•la•**ho**•ma

ok•ra

old

old•en

old-fash•ioned

Old Tes•ta•ment

O•**lym**•pics

om•**buds**•man

also pronounced
om•buds•man

om•e•let (*or*
om•e•lette)

o•men

om•i•nous

o•**mis**•sion

o•**mit**

o•**mit**•tance

o•**mit**•ted

opera

o•**mit**•ting

om•ni•bus

om•ni•vore

once

on•com•ing

one (sounds like "won")

One minute, please!

one-sid•ed

one-way

on•go•ing

on•ion

on-line

on•ly

on•o•mat•o•**poe**•ia

on•set

on•to

on•ward

on•wards

ooze

ooz•ing

o•pal

o•**paque**

o•pen

o•pen•ing

op•er•a

op•er•ate

op•er•**at**•ic

op•er•at•ing

op•er•**a**•tion

op•er•**a**•tion•al

op•er•a•tor

op•er•**et**•ta

oph•thal•**mol**•o•gist

oph•thal•**mol**•o•gy

o•**pin**•ion

o•**pin**•ion•at•ed

o•**pos**•sum

op•**po**•nent

op•por•**tu**•ni•ties

op•por•**tu**•ni•ty

op•**pose**

op•**pos**•ing

op•po•site

op•po•**si**•tion

op•**press**

opt

op•ti•cal

op•**ti**•cian

op•ti•mism

op•ti•mist

op•ti•**mis**•tic

op•ti•mum

op•tion

op•tion•al

op•**tom**•e•trist

or

o•ral (sounds like "aural")

An oral report is spoken.

or•ange

o•**rang**•u•tan

or•bit

or•chard

or•ches•tra

or•ches•**tra**•tion

or•chid

or•**dain**

or•**deal**

or•der

or•der•ly

or•di•nal

or•di•**nar**•i•ly

or•di•**nar**•y

ore

Or•e•gon

or•gan

or•**gan**•ic

or•**gan**•i•cal•ly

or•gan•ism

or•gan•ist

or•gan•i•**za**•tion

or•gan•ize

or•gan•iz•ing

o•ri•ent

o•ri•en•**ta**•tion

o•ri•**ga**•mi

or•i•gin

o•**rig**•i•nal

o•**rig**•i•nate

o•ri•ole

or•na•ment

or•na•**men**•tal

or•**nate**

or•ni•**thol**•o•gist

or•ni•**thol**•o•gy

or•phan

or•phan•age

or•tho•**don**•tist

or•tho•dox

or•tho•dox•y

os•**mo**•sis

os•trich

oth•er

oth•er•wise

ot•ter

ouch

ought

ounce

our

ours

our•**selves**

oust

out

out•break

out•burst

out•cast

out•come

out•cry

out•**dat**•ed

out•**do**

out•**doors**

out•er

out•fit

out•fit•ted

out•fit•ting

out•**go**•ing

out•**grow**

out•ing

out•law

out•let

out•line

out•look

out•**num**•ber

out-of-date

out•pa•tient

out•post

out•put

out•rage

out•**ra**•geous

out•right

out•set

out•**side** (adv. and prep.)

out•side (n.)

out•skirts

out•**smart**

out•**spo**•ken

out•**stand**•ing

out•ward

out•**wit**

out•**wit**•ted

out•**wit**•ting

o•val

o•va•ries

o•va•ry

o•**va**•tion

ov•en

o•ver

o•ver•**all**

o•ver•alls

o•ver•**bear**•ing

o•ver•board

o•ver•**came**

o•ver•cast

o•ver•coat

o•ver•**come**

o•ver•**com**•ing

o•ver•dose

o•ver•draft

o•ver•drawn

o•ver•**due**

o•ver•**eat**

o•ver•flow

o•ver•**grown**

o•ver•hand

o•ver•**haul**

o•ver•**head** (adv.)

o•ver•head (adj. and n.)

o•ver•**hear**

o•ver•**joyed**

o•ver•**lap**

o•ver•**lapped**

o•ver•**lap**•ping

o•ver•**load** (v.)

o•ver•load (n.)

o•ver•**look**

o•ver•ly

o•ver•**night** (adv.)

o•ver•night (adj.)

o•ver•pass

o•ver•**pop**•u•la•ted

o•ver•pop•u•**la**•tion

o•ver•**pow**•er

o•ver•**rat**•ed

o•ver•re•**ac**•tion

o•ver•**rule**

o•ver•**run**

o•ver•**run**•ning

o•ver•seas

o•ver•**sleep**

o•ver•**slept**

o•ver•**take**

o•ver•**throw**

o•ver•time

o•ver•ture

o•ver•**turn**

o•ver•weight

o•ver•**whelm**

o•ver•**work**

owe

owed (sounds like "ode")

I owed my brother two dollars.

ow•ing

owl

own

own•er

own•er•ship

ox

ox•i•**da**•tion

ox•i•dize

ox•i•diz•ing

ox•y•gen

ox•y•**mo**•ron

oy•ster

o•zone

pace
pace•mak•er
pach•y•derm
pa•**cif**•ic
Pa•**cif**•ic **O**•cean
pac•i•fied
pac•i•fi•er
pac•i•fies
pac•i•fism
pac•i•fist
pac•i•fy
pack
pack•age
pack•ag•ing
pack•et
pact
pad
pad•ded
pad•dies
pad•ding
pad•dle
pad•dy
pad•lock
pa•gan
page
pag•eant
pag•eant•ry
pag•er
pag•ing
pa•**go**•da
pail (sounds like "pale")

I knocked over the pail of water.
pain
pain•ful
pain•kill•er
pain•less
pains•tak•ing
paint
paint•brush
paint•er
pair (sounds like "pare" and "pear")
I lost a pair of socks.
pa•**ja**•mas
pal
pal•ace
pal•ate (sounds like "palette")

paddle

Peanut butter sticks to my palate.
pale (sounds like "pail")
She looks pale and sick.
pale•ness
pa•le•on•**tol**•o•gist
pa•le•on•**tol**•o•gy
Pa•le•o•**zo**•ic
Pal•es•tine
pal•ette (sounds like "palate")
The painter put bright colors on his palette.
pal•in•drome
pal•i•**sade**
palm
pal•**met**•to
palm•ist•ry
pal•o•**mi**•no
pam•pas
pam•per
pam•phlet
pan
pan•cake
pan•cre•as
pan•da
pan•de•**mo**•ni•um
pane
pan•el
pan•el•ist

pang
pan•ic
pan•icked
pan•ick•ing
pan•ick•y
pan•ic-**strick**•en
panned
pan•o•**ram**•a
pan•o•**ram**•ic
pan•sies
pan•sy
pant
pan•ther
pan•ties
pan•to•mime
pan•tries
pan•try
pants
pan•ty
pa•**pa**•ya
pa•per
pa•per•back
pa•per•weight
pa•per•work
pa•pier-mâ•**ché**
pa•**poose**
pap•**ri**•ka
  also pronounced
  pap•ri•ka
pa•**py**•rus
par
par•a•ble
par•a•chute
par•a•chut•ing

pa•**rade**
pa•**rad**•ing
par•a•dise
par•a•dox
par•a•**dox**•i•cal
par•af•fin
par•a•graph
par•a•keet
par•a•**le**•gal
par•al•lel
par•al•**lel**•o•gram
pa•**ral**•y•sis
par•a•lyze
par•a•lyz•ing
par•a•**me**•ci•a (pl.)
par•a•**me**•ci•um
  (sing.)
par•a•mount
par•a•pher•**na**•lia
par•a•phrase
par•a•phras•ing

parachuting

par•a•**ple**•gic
par•a•site
par•a•**sit**•ic
par•a•sol
par•a•troop•er
par•cel
parch
parch•ment
par•don
pare (sounds like "pair"
  and "pear")
  Use a knife to pare
  the apple.
par•ent
pa•**ren**•the•ses (pl.)
pa•**ren**•the•sis (sing.)
par•ing
par•ish
pa•**rish**•ion•er
park
par•ka
park•way
par•lia•ment
par•lia•**men**•ta•ry
par•lor
Par•me•san
pa•**ro**•chi•al
par•o•dies
par•o•dy
pa•**role**
par•rot
pars•ley
pars•nip
par•son

part
Par•the•non
par•tial
par•ti•al•i•ty
par•tic•i•pant
par•tic•i•pate
par•tic•i•pat•ing
par•tic•i•pa•tion
par•ti•ci•ple
par•ti•cle
par•tic•u•lar
par•ties
part•ing
par•ti•tion
part•ly
part•ner
par•tridge
part-time
par•ty
pass
pas•sage
pas•sage•way
pas•sen•ger
pas•ser•by
pas•sion
pas•sion•ate
pas•sive
Pass•o•ver
pass•port
pass•word
past
pas•ta
paste
pas•tel

pas•teur•i•za•tion
pas•teur•ize
pas•ti•er
pas•ti•est
pas•time
pas•ti•ness
pas•tor
pas•tor•al
pas•try
pas•ture
pat
patch
patch•work
patch•y
pâ•té
pat•ent
pat•er•nal
pat•er•ni•ty
path
pa•thet•ic
pa•thet•i•cal•ly
path•o•log•i•cal
pa•thol•o•gist
pa•thol•o•gy
pa•tience
pa•tient
pat•i•o
pat•i•os
pa•tri•arch
pa•tri•ot
pa•tri•ot•ic
pa•tri•ot•ism
pa•trol
pa•trolled

pa•trol•ling
pa•tron
pa•tron•age
pa•tron•ize
pa•tron•iz•ing
pat•ted
pat•ter
pat•tern
pat•ties
pat•ting
pat•ty
pau•per
pause
paus•ing
pave
pave•ment
pa•vil•ion
pav•ing
paw
pawn
pawn•brok•er
pay
pay•roll
pea
peace (sounds like "piece")
The countries signed a peace treaty.
peace•a•ble
peace•ful
peace•ful•ly
peace•mak•er
peace•time

peach

pea•cock

peak (sounds like
"peek")
*She's at the peak
of her game.*

peal (sounds like
"peel")
*At noon, the bells
peal.*

pea•nut

pea•nut **but**•ter

pear (sounds like "pair"
and "pare")
*You eat the pear, and
I'll eat the apple.*

pearl

peas•ant

peat

peb•ble

pe•can
also pronounced
pe•**can**

peck

pe•**cu**•liar

pe•cu•li•**ar**•i•ties

pe•cu•li•**ar**•i•ty

ped•al (sounds like
"peddle")
Pedal the bike slowly.

ped•dle (sounds like
"pedal")
*Can I peddle this for
two dollars?*

ped•dler

ped•dling

ped•es•tal

pe•**des**•tri•an

pe•di•a•**tric**•ian

ped•i•gree

peek (sounds like
"peak")
*Don't peek behind
the door.*

peel (sounds like
"peal")
Peel the apple, please.

peep

peer (sounds like
"pier")
*Your classmate is
your peer.*

peg

Pe•king•**ese**

pel•i•can

pel•let

pell-mell

pelt

pen

pe•nal•ize

pen•al•ties

pen•al•ty

pen•cil

pen•dant

pen•du•lum

pen•e•trate

pen•e•trat•ing

pen•e•**tra**•tion

pen•guin

pen•i•**cil**•lin

pen•**in**•su•la

pen•i•tence

pen•i•tent

pen•i•**ten**•tia•ries

pen•i•**ten**•tia•ry

pen•knife

pen•knives

pen name

pen•nant

pen•nies

pen•ni•less

pen•ning

Penn•syl•**va**•nia

pen•ny

pen pal

pen•sion

pen•ta•gon

pen•**tag**•o•nal

pent•house

pe•o•ny

peo•ple

pep

pepped

pep•per

pep•per•mint

pep•per•y

pep•ping

per (sounds like
"purr")
*They charge a dime
per apple.*

per•**ceive**

per•**ceiv**•ing

per•**cent**
per•**cent**•age
per•**cep**•ti•ble
per•**cep**•tion
per•**cep**•tive
perch
per•**chance**
per•**cus**•sion
per•**cus**•sion•ist
per•**en**•nial
per•e•**stroi**•ka
per•fect (adj.)
per•**fect** (v.)
per•**fec**•tion
per•**form**
per•**form**•ance
per•**form**•er
per•fume
  also pronounced
  per•**fume**
per•**haps**
per•il
per•i•lous
pe•**rim**•e•ter
pe•ri•od
pe•ri•**od**•ic
pe•ri•**od**•i•cal
pe•**riph**•er•al
pe•**riph**•er•ies
pe•**riph**•er•y
per•i•scope
per•ish
per•ish•a•ble
per•jure

per•ju•ry
perk
perk•y
perm
per•ma•nence
per•ma•nent
per•me•ate
per•**mis**•si•ble
per•**mis**•sion
per•**mis**•sive
per•**mis**•sive•ness
per•**mit** (v.)
per•mit (n.)
per•**mit**•ted
per•**mit**•ting
per•mu•**ta**•tion
per•pen•**dic**•u•lar
per•**pet**•u•al
per•**pet**•u•ate

periscope

per•**pet**•u•at•ing
per•**plex**
per•**plex**•i•ties
per•**plex**•i•ty
per•se•cute
per•se•cut•ing
per•se•**cu**•tion
per•se•**ver**•ance
per•se•**vere**
per•se•**ver**•ing
Per•sia
per•**sim**•mon
per•**sist**
per•**sist**•ence
per•**sist**•ent
per•son
per•son•al
per•son•**al**•i•ties
per•son•**al**•i•ty
per•son•al•ly
per•son•**nel**
per•**spec**•tive
per•spi•**ra**•tion
per•**spire**
per•**spir**•ing
per•**suade**
per•**suad**•ing
per•**sua**•sion
per•**sua**•sive
per•**tain**
per•ti•nent
per•**turb**
Pe•**ru**
per•**verse**

per•**ver**•si•ty
pe•**se**•ta
pe•so
pes•si•mism
pes•si•mist
pes•si•**mis**•tic
pest
pes•ter
pes•ti•cide
pes•tle
pet
pet•al
pe•**ti**•tion
pet•ri•fied
pe•**tro**•le•um
pet•ti•coat
pet•ting
pet•ty
pe•**tu**•nia
pew
pew•ter
phan•tom
phar•aoh
phar•ma•cies
phar•ma•cist
phar•ma•cy
phase
pheas•ant
phe•**nom**•e•na
phe•**nom**•e•nal
phe•**nom**•e•non
phe•**nom**•e•nons
phil•**an**•thro•pist
phil•**an**•thro•py

phil•o•**den**•dron
phil•o•**soph**•i•cal
phi•**los**•o•phy
phlegm
pho•bi•a
pho•bic
phone
pho•**net**•i•cal•ly
pho•**net**•ics
pho•no•graph
phos•pho•**res**•cence
phos•pho•**res**•cent
phos•pho•rus
pho•to
pho•to•cop•i•er
pho•to•cop•ies
pho•to•cop•y
pho•to•cop•y•ing
pho•to•**gen**•ic
pho•to•graph
pho•**to**•gra•pher
pho•to•**graph**•ic
pho•**to**•gra•phy
pho•to•**jour**•nal•ism
pho•to•**jour**•nal•ist
pho•to•**syn**•the•sis
phrase
phys•i•cal
phy•**si**•cian
phys•i•cist
phys•ics
pi (sounds like "pie")
 π *stands for pi*
 in math.

pi•**an**•ist
 also pronounced
 pi•a•nist

(**piano**)

pi•**an**•o
pi•**an**•os
pic•co•lo
pic•co•los
pick
pick•ax (*or* **pick**•axe)
pick•er•el
pick•et
pick•et•er
pick•i•er
pick•i•est
pick•le
pick•pock•et
pick•up

pick•y
pic•nic
pic•nicked
pic•nick•ing
pic•to•graph
pic•**to**•ri•al
pic•ture
pic•tur•**esque**
pie (sounds like "pi")

Cherry pie is my favorite dessert.

piece (sounds like "peace")

May I have a piece of pie?

piece•work
pier (sounds like "peer")

Don't stand on the edge of the pier.

pierce
pierc•ing
pi•e•ty
pig
pi•geon
pig•gy•back
pig•gy **bank**
pig•ment
pig•pen
pig•sties
pig•sty
pig•tail
pike
pile

pil•grim
pil•grim•age
pill
pil•lar
pil•low
pil•low•case
pi•lot
pim•ple
pin
pi•**ña**•ta
pin•ball
pin•cer
pinch
pin•cush•ion
pine
pine•ap•ple
Ping-Pong
pin•ing
pink
pink•eye
pin•point
pin•stripe
pint
pin•to
pin•tos
pin•wheel
pi•o•**neer**
pi•ous
pipe
pipe•line
pip•ing
pi•rate
pi•rat•ing
pis•**ta**•chio

pis•til (sounds like "pistol")

The pistil is the female part of the flower.

pis•tol (sounds like "pistil")

Did you hear a pistol shot?

pis•ton
pit
pi•ta
pitch
pitch•er
pitch•fork
pit•fall
pit•ied
pit•ies
pit•i•ful
pit•i•less
pit•ted
pit•y
pit•y•ing
piv•ot
piv•ot•al
pix•el
pix•ie (*or* pix•y)
pix•ies
piz•za
pla•cate
pla•cat•ing
place
plac•id
plac•ing
pla•gia•rism

pla•gia•rist

pla•gia•rize

pla•gia•riz•ing

plague

pla•guing

plaid

plain (sounds like "plane")

I like things plain, not fancy.

plain•tive

plait

plan

plane (sounds like "plain")

The plane was delayed by fog.

plan•et

plan•e•tar•i•um

plan•e•tar•y

plank

plank•ton

planned

plan•ning

plant

plan•tain

plan•ta•tion

plaque

plas•ma

plas•ter

plas•ter•er

plas•tic

plate

pla•teau

plate•let

plat•form

plat•ing

plat•i•num

Pla•to

pla•toon

plat•ter

plat•y•pus

plau•si•ble

play

play•er

play•ful

play•ful•ly

play•ground

play•mate

play•pen

play•room

play•wright

pla•za

plea

plead

pleas•ant

please

pleased

pleas•ing

pleas•ur•a•ble

pleas•ure

pleat

pleat•ed

pledge

pledg•ing

plen•ti•ful

plen•ty

pli•a•ble

pli•ers

plight

plod

plot

plo•ver

plow

pluck

pluck•i•ly

pluck•i•ness

pluck•y

plug

plugged

plug•ging

plum (sounds like "plumb")

I ate a small, ripe plum.

plum•age

plumb (sounds like "plum")

I felt plumb stupid.

plumb•er

plumb•ing

plume

plump

plun•der

plun•der•er

plunge

plung•ing

plu•ral

plus

Plu•to

plu•to•ni•um

ply•wood

pneu•**mat**•ic

pneu•**mo**•nia

poach

poach•er

pock•et

pock•et•book

pock•et•knife

pod

po•em

po•et

po•**et**•ic

po•et•ry

poin•**set**•ti•a

point

point-blank

point•less

point of view

poise

poised

poi•son

poi•son **i**•vy

poi•son•ous

poi•son **su**•mac

poke

pok•er

po•lar

pole (sounds like "poll")

She hitched her pony to the pole.

pole•cat

pole vault

po•**lice**

po•**lice**•man

po•**lice of**•fi•cer

po•**lice**•wom•an

pol•i•cies

pol•i•cy

po•li•o

pol•ish

pol•ished

po•**lite**

po•**lite**•ness

pol•i•**ti**•cian

pol•i•tics

pol•ka

pol•ka **dot**

poll (sounds like "pole")

The poll showed he would win the election.

pol•len

pol•li•nate

pol•li•nat•ing

pol•li•**na**•tion

pol•**lut**•ant

pol•**lute**

pol•**lut**•er

pol•**lut**•ing

pol•**lu**•tion

po•lo

pol•y•**es**•ter

pol•y•gon

pol•y•mer

pol•yp

pol•y•**sty**•rene

pol•y•un•**sat**•u•rates

pomp

pomp•ous

pon•cho

pond

pon•der

pon•der•ous

po•ny

Po•ny Ex•**press**

po•ny•tail

poo•dle

poodle

pool

poor (sounds like "pore" and "pour")

Once I was poor; now I'm rich.

poor•ly

pop

pop•corn

pope

pop•lar

pop•py
pop•u•lar
pop•u•**lar**•i•ty
pop•u•lar•ly
pop•u•late
pop•u•lat•ing
pop•u•**la**•tion
por•ce•lain
porch
por•cu•pine
pore (sounds like
  "poor" and "pour")
  *A pore is a tiny hole
  in your skin.*
pork
po•rous
por•poise
por•ridge
port
port•a•ble
por•ter
port•**fol**•i•o
port•hole
por•tion
port•ly
por•trait
por•**tray**
por•**tray**•al
pose
posh
pos•ing
po•**si**•tion
pos•i•tive
pos•se

pos•**sess**
pos•**ses**•sion
pos•**ses**•sive
pos•si•**bil**•i•ty
pos•si•ble
pos•sum

possum

post
post•age
post•al
post•card
post•er
post•hu•mous
post•man
post•mark
post•mast•er
post•mis•tress
post of•fice

post•**pone**
post•**pone**•ment
post•**pon**•ing
post•script
pos•ture
post•**war**
pot
po•**tas**•si•um
po•**ta**•to
po•**ta**•toes
po•ten•cy
po•tent
po•**ten**•tial
pot•hole
pot•ter
pot•ter•y
pouch
poul•try
pounce
pounc•ing
pound
pour (sounds like
  "poor" and "pore")
  *Please pour me
  some milk.*
pout
pov•er•ty
pow•der
pow•der•y
pow•er
pow•er•ful
pow•er•less
prac•ti•cal
prac•ti•**cal**•i•ty

prac•ti•cal•ly
prac•tice
prac•tic•ing
prai•rie
prai•rie **schoo**•ner
praise
prais•ing
prance
pranc•ing
prank
pray (sounds like
   "prey")

*Let's pray it won't
rain on our picnic.*

pray•er
pray•ing **man**•tis
preach
pre•**car**•i•ous
pre•**cau**•tion
pro•**code**
pre•ce•dence
pre•ce•dent
pre•**ced**•ing
pre•cinct
pre•cious
prec•i•pice
pre•**cip**•i•tate
pre•**cip**•i•tating
pre•cip•i•**ta**•tion
pre•**cise**
pre•**cise**•ly
pre•**co**•cious
pred•a•tor
pred•e•ces•sor

pre•**dic**•a•ment
pred•i•cate
pre•**dict**
pre•**dic**•tion
pre•**dom**•i•nate
pre•**dom**•i•nat•ing
preen
pre•face
pre•**fer**
pref•er•ence
pre•**ferred**
pre•**fer**•ring
pre•fix
preg•nan•cy
preg•nant
pre•his•**tor**•ic
pre•**his**•tor•y
prej•u•dice
pre•**lim**•i•nar•y
pre•ma•**ture**
pre•**med**•i•tat•ed
pre•**mier** (sounds like
   "premiere")

*The French
government has a
new premier.*

pre•**miere** (sounds like
   "premier")

*Many famous movie
stars attended the
premiere.*

prem•ise
prem•is•es
pre•mi•um

pre•mo•**ni**•tion
pre•**oc**•cu•pied
prep•a•**ra**•tion
pre•**pare**
pre•**par**•ing
prep•o•**si**•tion
pre•**pos**•ter•ous
prep school
pre•school
pre•**scribe**
pre•**scrib**•ing
pre•**scrip**•tion
pres•ence
pre•sent (n.)
pre•**sent** (v.)
pres•en•**ta**•tion
pres•ent•ly
pre•**serv**•a•tive
pre•**serve**
pre•**serv**•ing
pre•side
pres•i•den•cy
pres•i•dent
pres•i•dent-e•**lect**
pres•i•**den**•tial
pre•**sid**•ing
press
pres•sing
pres•sure
pres•sur•ing
pres•sur•ize
pres•sur•iz•ing
pres•**tige**
pres•**ti**•gious

pre•**sum**•a•bly
pre•**sume**
pre•**sum**•ing
pre•**sump**•tion
pre•**tend**
pre•tense
  also pronounced
  pre•**tense**
pre•text
pret•ti•er
pret•ti•est
pret•ti•ly
pret•ti•ness
pret•ty
pret•zel
pre•**vail**
prev•a•lent
pre•**vent**
pre•**ven**•tion
pre•**ven**•tive
pre•view
pre•vi•ous
prey (sounds like
  "pray")
  Owls often prey
  on mice.
price
price•less
pric•ing
prick
prick•le
prick•ly
pride
pried

pries
priest
priest•hood
priest•ly
prim
pri•ma **don**•na
pri•**mar**•i•ly
pri•mar•y
pri•mate
prime
pri•**me**•val
prim•i•tive
prim•rose
prince
prince•ly
prin•cess
prin•ci•pal (sounds like
  "principle")
  The principal is in
  the office.
prin•ci•ple (sounds like
  "principal")
  Please explain the
  principle of gravity.
print
print•out
pri•or
pri•**or**•i•ties
pri•**or**•i•ty
prism
pris•on
pris•on•er
pri•va•cy
pri•vate

priv•i•lege
prize
pro
prob•a•**bil**•i•ty
prob•a•ble
pro•bate
pro•bat•ing
pro•**ba**•tion
probe
prob•ing
prob•lem
pro•**ce**•dure
pro•**ceed**
pro•ceeds
proc•ess
pro•**ces**•sion
proc•es•sor
pro•**claim**
proc•la•**ma**•tion
pro•**cras**•ti•nate
pro•**cras**•ti•nat•ing
pro•cras•ti•**na**•tion
pro•**cras**•ti•na•tor
prod
prod•ded
prod•ding
prod•i•gal
prod•i•gies
prod•i•gy
pro•**duce** (v.)
pro•duce (n.)
pro•**duc**•er
pro•**duc**•ing
prod•uct

pro•**duc**•tion
pro•**duc**•tive
pro•duc•**tiv**•i•ty
pro•**fess**
pro•**fes**•sion
pro•**fes**•sion•al
pro•**fes**•sor
pro•**fi**•cien•cy
pro•**fi**•cient
pro•file
pro•fit (sounds like
   "prophet")
   We made a profit
   on our car wash.

propeller

prof•it•a•ble
pro•**found**
pro•gram
pro•grammed
pro•gram•mer
pro•gram•ming
prog•ress
pro•**gres**•sion
pro•**gress**•ive
pro•**hib**•it
pro•hi•**bi**•tion
proj•ect (n.)
pro•**ject** (v.)
pro•**jec**•tile
pro•**jec**•tion
pro•**jec**•tor
pro•**li**•fic
pro•logue
pro•**long**
prom•e•**nade**

prom•e•**nad**•ing
prom•ise
prom•ised
prom•ises
prom•is•ing
pro•**mote**
pro•**mot**•ing
pro•**mo**•tion
prompt
prompt•er
prone
prong
pro•noun
pro•**nounce**
pro•**nounce**•ment
pro•**nounc**•ing
pro•nun•ci•**a**•tion
proof
proof•read
prop

prop•a•**gan**•da
pro•**pel**
pro•**pel**•lant
pro•**pelled**
pro•**pel**•ler
pro•**pel**•ling
prop•er
prop•er•ly
prop•er•ties
prop•er•ty
proph•e•cies
proph•e•cy
proph•et (sounds
   like "profit")
   The prophet predicted
   war, then peace.
pro•**por**•tion
pro•**por**•tion•al
pro•**pos**•al
pro•**pose**
pro•**pos**•ing
pro•po•**si**•tion
pro•**pul**•sion
prose
pros•e•cute
pros•e•**cu**•tion
pros•e•cu•tor
pros•pect
pro•**spec**•tive
pros•pec•tor
pro•**spec**•tus
pros•per
pros•**per**•i•ty
pros•per•ous

pro•**tect**
pro•**tec**•tion
pro•**tec**•tive
pro•**tec**•tor
pro•tein
pro•test (n.)
pro•**test** (v.)
Prot•es•tant
pro•ton
pro•to•plasm
pro•to•type
pro•to•**zo**•a
pro•to•**zo**•an
pro•**trac**•tor
proud
prove
prov•erb
pro•**vide**
pro•**vid**•er
pro•**vid**•ing
prov•ince
pro•**vin**•cial
prov•ing
pro•**vi**•sion
pro•**voke**
pro•**vok**•ing
prowl
prox•**im**•i•ty
pru•dence
pru•dent
prune
prun•ing
pry
psalm

pseu•do•nym
psy•**chi**•a•trist
psy•**chi**•a•try
psy•chic
psy•cho•**log**•i•cal
psy•**chol**•o•gist
psy•**chol**•o•gy
psy•cho•path
pter•o•**dac**•tyl
pub
pu•ber•ty
pub•lic
pub•li•**ca**•tion
pub•li•cist
pub•**lic**•i•ty
pub•li•cize
pub•li•ciz•ing
pub•lic•ly
pub•lish
pub•lish•er
puck
puck•er
pud•ding
pud•dle
pueb•lo
puff
puf•fin
puf•fy
pug
pug•**na**•cious
pull
pul•ley
pull•o•ver
pulp

pul•pit
pul•sate
pul•sat•ing
pul•**sa**•tion
pu•ma
pum•mel
pump
pump•er•nic•kel
pump•kin

pumpkin

pun
punch
punc•tu•al
punc•tu•**al**•i•ty
punc•tu•**a**•tion
punc•ture
punc•tur•ing
pun•gent
pun•ish

pun•ish•ment

punk

punt

pu•ny

pu•pa (sing.)

pu•pae (pl.)

pu•pil

pup•pet

pup•py

pur•chase

pur•chas•er

pur•chas•ing

pure

pure•bred

pu•**ree**

purge

purg•ing

pu•ri•fi•**ca**•tion

pu•ri•fied

pu•ri•fies

pu•ri•fy

Pur•i•tan

pu•ri•ty

pur•ple

pur•pose

purr (sounds like "per")

*Do you hear the
happy cat purr?*

purse

purs•ing

pur•**sue**

pur•**su**•er

pur•**su**•ing

pur•**suit**

pus

push

push•er

push•ov•er

push-up

pus•sy

put

pu•trid

putt

put•ler

put•ting

put•ty

puz•zle

puz•zling

py•lon

pyr•a•mid

Q

quack
quad
quad•ran•gle
quad•rant
quad•ri•**lat**•er•al
quad•ru•ped
qua•**dru**•ple
qua•**dru**•plet
quag•mire
quail
quaint
quaint•ness
quake
Quak•er
quak•ing
qual•i•fi•**ca**•tion
qual•i•fied
qual•i•fies
qual•i•fy
qual•i•ties
qual•i•ty
qualm
quan•dar•ies
quan•dar•y
quan•ti•ties
quan•ti•ty
quar•an•tine
quark
quar•rel
quar•rel•some
quar•ries
quar•ry

quart
quar•ter
quar•ter•back
quart•er•ly
quar•**tet**
quartz
qua•sar
qua•ver
quay (sounds like "key")

The boats are unloaded at the quay.

quea•si•er
quea•si•est
quea•si•ness
quea•sy
Que•**bec**
queen

queen

queer
quench
que•ries
que•ry
quest
ques•tion
ques•tion•**naire**
quet•**zal**
queue (sounds like "cue")

We stood in a queue to get on the bus.

quib•ble
quib•bling
quiche
quick
quick•en
quick•ly
quick•sand
quick•sil•ver
quick-tem•pered
quick-wit•ted
qui•et
qui•et•ly
qui•et•ness
quill
quilt
quilt•ed
qui•nine
quin•**tet**
quin•**tup**•let
quip

quipped

quirk

quirk•i•ness

quir•ky

quit

quite

quit•ting

quiv•er

quiz

quizzed

quiz•zes

quiz•zi•cal

quiz•zing

quo•rum

quo•ta

quot•a•ble

quo•ta•tion

quote

quo•tient

quot•ing

Qur'•an (*or* Ko•ran)

rab•bi
rab•bit
ra•bies
rac•**coon**
race
race•track
ra•cial
rac•ing
rac•ist
rack
rack•et (*or* rac•quet)
rac•quet•ball
ra•dar
ra•di•al
ra•di•ance
ra•di•ant
ra•di•ate
ra•di•at•ing
ra•di•**a**•tion
ra•di•**a**•tor
rad•i•cal
ra•di•i
ra•di•o
ra•di•o•**ac**•tive
ra•di•o•ac•**tiv**•i•ty
rad•ish
ra•di•um
ra•di•us
ra•don
raf•fle
raft
rag

rage
rag•ged
rag•ged•y
rag•ing
rag•weed
raid
rail
rail•ing
rail•road
rail•way
rain (sounds like
   "reign" and "rein")
   Rain is falling.
rain•bow
rain•coat
rain•drop
rain•fall
rain•y
raise
rai•sin
rais•ing
rake
rak•ing
ral•lies
ral•ly
ral•ly•ing
ram
RAM
Ram•a•dan
ram•ble
ram•bling
ramp

ram•page
ram•pant
ram•part
ram•shack•le
ran
ranch
ran•cid
ran•dom
rang
range
rang•er
rank
ran•sack
ran•som
rant
rap (sounds like
   "wrap")
   We love rap songs.
rap•id
rap•ids
rapped
rap•per
rap•ping
rapt
rare
ras•cal
rash
rasp
rasp•ber•ry
rat
rate
rath•er

rat•i•fi•**ca**•tion
rat•i•fied
rat•i•fies
rat•i•fy
ra•ti•o
ra•tion
ra•tion•al
ra•ti•os
rat•tle
rat•tler
rat•tle•snake
rau•cous
rave
ra•vel
ra•ven
rav•en•ous
ra•**vine**
rav•ing
raw
ray
ray•on
ra•zor
reach
re•**act**
re•**act**•ion
re•**ac**•tor
read
read•a•ble
read•i•ly
read•y
real
re•al•**is**•tic
re•**al**•i•ties
re•**al**•i•ty

re•al•i•**za**•tion
re•al•ize
re•al•iz•ing
re•al•ly
  also pronounced
  real•ly
reap
re•ap•**pear**
re•ap•**pear**•ance
rear
re•ar•**range**
re•ar•**rang**•ing
rea•son
rea•son•a•ble
rea•son•a•bly
rea•son•ing
re•as•**sign**
re•as•**sign**•ing
re•as•**sur**•ance
re•as•**sure**
re•as•**sur**•ing

(read)

re•**bel** (v.)
re•bel (n.)
re•**bel**•lion
re•**bel**•lious
re•**boot**
re•**but**
re•**but**•tal
re•**but**•ted
re•**call** (v.)
re•**call** (n.)
  also pronounced
  re•call
re•cap
re•**cede**
re•**ced**•ing
re•**ceipt**
re•**ceive**
re•**ceiv**•er
re•**ceiv**•ing
re•cent
re•**cep**•ta•cle
re•**cep**•tion
re•**cep**•tion•ist
re•cess
  also pronounced
  re•**cess**
re•**ces**•sion
rec•i•pe
re•**cit**•al
re•**cite**
reck•less
reck•on
re•**claim**
re•**cline**

re•**clin**•ing
rec•og•**niz**•a•ble
rec•og•nize
rec•og•niz•ing
re•col•**lect**
rec•ol•**lec**•tion
rec•om•**mend**
rec•om•men•**da**•tion
re•con•**sid**•er
re•con•**struct**
re•con•**struc**•tion
re•**cord** (v.)
rec•ord (n.)
re•**cord**•er
re•**cord**•ing
re•**cov**•er
rec•re•**a**•tion
rec•re•**a**•tion•al
re•**cruit**
re•**cruit**•ment
rec•tan•gle
rec•**tan**•gu•lar
re•**cu**•per•ate
re•**cu**•per•at•ing
re•**cy**•cla•ble
re•**cy**•cle
re•**cy**•cling
red
red•coat
red•den
red•dish
re•**deem**
re•**demp**•tion
re•de•**sign**•ed

red-hand•ed
re•**duce**
re•**duc**•ing
re•**duc**•tion
red•wood
reed
reef
reek (sounds like
"wreak")
*Did the house reek
of onion?*
reel
re•e•**lect**
re•e•**lec**•tion
re•**en**•tries
re•**en**•try
re•**fer**
ref•er•**ee**
ref•er•ence
ref•er•**en**•dum
re•**fer**•ral
re•**ferred**
re•**fer**•ring
re•**fill** (v.)
re•fill (n.)
re•**fine**
re•**fined**
re•**fin**•er•ies
re•**fin**•er•y
re•**fin**•ing
re•**flect**
re•**flec**•tion
re•**flec**•tive
re•**flec**•tor

re•flex
re•**for**•est
re•for•est•**a**•tion
re•**form**
ref•or•**ma**•tion
re•**for**•ma•tor•ies
re•**for**•ma•tor•y
re•**form**•ing
re•**fract**
re•**frac**•tion
re•**frain**
re•**fresh**
re•**fresh**•ments
re•**frig**•er•ate
re•**frig**•er•**a**•tion
re•**frig**•er•a•tor
re•**fu**•el
re•**fuge**
ref•u•**gee**
  also pronounced
  ref•u•gee
re•**fund** (v.)

reflection

re•fund (n.)
re•**fus**•al
re•**fuse**
ref•use
re•**fus**•ing
re•gal
re•**gard**
re•**gard**•ing
re•**gard**•less
re•**gards**
reg•gae
re•**gime**
reg•i•ment
re•gion
re•gion•al
reg•is•ter
reg•is•**tra**•tion
re•**gret**
re•**gret**•ful
re•**gret**•ta•ble
re•**gret**•ta•bly
reg•u•lar
reg•u•**lar**•i•ty
reg•u•late
reg•u•lat•ing
reg•u•**la**•tion
re•**gur**•gi•tate
re•**hears**•al
re•**hearse**
re•**hears**•ing
reign (sounds like
   "rain" and "rein")
   *The king's reign lasted
   fifty years.*

re•im•**burse**
re•im•**burs**•ing
rein (sounds like "rain"
   and "reign")
   Hold the horse's rein.
rein•deer
re•in•**force**
re•in•**force**•ment
re•in•**forc**•ing
re•**ject** (v.)
re•ject (n.)
re•**jec**•tion
re•**joice**
re•**joic**•ing
re•**late**
re•**lat**•ing
re•**la**•tion
re•**la**•tion•ship
rel•a•tive
rel•a•tive•ly
re•**lax**
re•lax•**a**•tion
re•lay
re•**lease**
re•**leas**•ing
re•**lent**
re•**lent**•less
rel•e•vance
rel•e•vant
re•li•a•**bil**•i•ty
re•**li**•a•ble
re•**li**•a•bly
re•lic
re•**lied**

re•**lief**
re•**lies**
re•**lieve**
re•**lig**•ion
re•**li**•gious
re•lish
re•**luct**•ant
re•**ly**
re•**main**
re•**main**•der
re•**mains**
re•**mark**
re•**mark**•a•ble
re•**mark**•a•bly
re•**me**•di•al
rem•e•dies
rem•e•dy
re•**mem**•ber
re•**mem**•brance
re•**mind**
re•**mind**•er
re•**mod**•el
re•**morse**
re•**morse**•ful
re•**mote**
re•**mote**•ness
re•**move**
re•**mov**•ing
Re•nais•sance
ren•dez•vous
re•**new**
re•**new**•a•ble
ren•o•vate
ren•o•vat•ing

ren•o•**va**•tion
re•**nown**
re•**nowned**
rent
rent•al
re•**paid**
re•**pair**
re•**pay**
re•**pay**•ment
re•**peal**
re•**peat**
re•**pel**
re•**pelled**
re•**pel**•lent
re•**pel**•ling
re•**pent**
re•**pent**•ance
re•**pent**•ant
re•per•**cus**•sion
rep•er•toire
rep•e•**ti**•tion
rep•e•**ti**•tious
re•**pet**•i•tive
re•**place**
re•**place**•ment
re•**plac**•ing
re•**play** (v.)
re•play (n.)
re•**plen**•ish
rep•li•ca
rep•li•cate
re•**plied**
re•**plies**
re•**ply**

re•**ply**•ing
re•**port**
re•**port**•er
rep•re•**sent**
rep•re•sen•**ta**•tion
rep•re•**sent**•a•tive
re•**press**
re•**pres**•sion
re•**prieve**
rep•ri•mand
re•pro•**duce**
re•pro•**duc**•ing
re•pro•**duc**•tion
rep•tile
rep•**til**•i•an
re•**pub**•lic
re•**pub**•li•can
re•**pulse**
re•**pul**•sive
rep•u•ta•ble
rep•u•**ta**•tion
re•**quest**
re•**qui**•em
re•**quire**
re•**quire**•ment
re•**quir**•ing
re•**read**
re•**run** (v.)
re•run (n.)
res•cue
res•cu•er
re•**search**
  also pronounced
  re•search

re•**sem**•ble
re•**sem**•bling
re•**sent**
re•**sent**•ment
res•er•**va**•tion
re•**serve**
re•**served**
re•**serv**•ing
re•ser•voir
re•**side**
res•i•dence
res•i•dent
res•i•**den**•tial
res•i•due
re•**sign**
res•ig•**na**•tion
re•**signed**
re•**sign**•ing
res•in
re•**sist**
re•**sis**•tance
re•**sis**•tant
res•o•**lu**•tion
re•**solve**
re•**solv**•ing
re•**sort**
re•**source**
  also pronounced
  re•source
re•**source**•ful
re•**spect**
re•**spect**•a•ble
re•**spect**•ful
re•**spec**•tive

res•pi•**ra**•tion

res•pi•ra•to•ry

re•**spond**

re•**sponse**

re•spon•si•**bil**•i•ties

re•spon•si•**bil**•i•ty

re•**spon**•si•ble

re•**spon**•si•bly

rest

res•tau•rant

rest•less

res•to•**ra**•tion

re•**store**

re•**stor**•ing

re•**strain**

re•**straint**

re•**strict**

re•**stric**•tion

re•**stric**•tive

re•**sult**

re•**sume** (often
confused with
"resumé")

*Please resume what
you were doing.*

re•su•mé (often
confused with
"resume")

*My resumé lists all
my jobs.*

re•**sus**•ci•tate

re•**sus**•ci•tat•ing

re•sus•ci•**ta**•tion

re•**sus**•ci•ta•tor

re•tail

re•tail•er

re•**tain**

re•**tard**

re•tar•**da**•tion

ret•i•na

re•**tire**

restaurant

re•**tir**•ing

re•**trace**

re•**treat**

re•**triev**•a•ble

re•**triev**•al

re•**trieve**

re•**triev**•er

re•**triev**•ing

re•**turn**

re•**un**•ion

re•**us**•a•ble

rev

re•**veal**

rev•e•**la**•tion

re•**venge**

rev•e•nue

re•**ver**•ber•ate

rev•er•ence

rev•er•ent

re•**ver**•sal

re•**verse**

re•**vers**•ing

re•**vert**

re•**view**

re•**vise**

re•**vis**•ing

re•**vi**•sion

re•**vive**

re•**viv**•ing

re•**voke**

re•**vok**•ing

re•**volt**

re•**volt**•ing

rev•o•**lu**•tion

rev•o•**lu**•tion•ar•y

re•**volve**

re•**volv**•er

re•**volv**•ing

re•**ward**

re•**ward**•ing

re•**word**

rheu•**mat**•ic **fe**•ver

rheu•ma•tism

rhi•**noc**•er•os

Rhode **Is**•land

rho•do•**den**•dron

rhom·bus
rhu·barb
rhyme
rhym·ing
rhythm
rib
rib·bon
rice
rich
rick·et·y
rick·sha (*or* rick·shaw)
ric·o·chet
rid
rid·dle
ride
ridge
rid·i·cule
ri·**dic**·u·lous
ri·fle
rig
rig·a·ma·role
rigged
rig·ging
right (sounds like "write")
  Turn right.
right·eous
right-**hand**·ed
rig·id
ri·**gid**·i·ty
rim
rind
ring (sounds like "wring")

I think I heard the phone ring.
ring·lead·er
ring·let
rink
rinse
Ri·o **Gran**·de
ri·ot
rip
ripe

(robot)

ripped
rip·ping
rip·ple
rise
risk
rit·u·al
ri·val
ri·val·ry
riv·er

road (sounds like "rode" and "rowed")
  The truck drove down the road.
road·run·ner
road·side
roam
roar
roast
rob
rob·ber·y
robe
rob·in
ro·bot
ro·**bot**·ic
ro·**bot**·ics
ro·**bust**
rock
rock·et
rock·ing
rock 'n' roll
rod
rode (sounds like "road" and "rowed")
  She rode her horse.
ro·dent
ro·de·o
  also pronounced ro·**de**·o
roe (sounds like "row")
  Roe are fish eggs.
rogue
role (sounds like "roll")
  She landed a good role in the movie.

roll (sounds like "role")
  Did you eat my roll?
rol•ler
rol•ler **coast**•er
rol•ler-skate (v.)
rol•ler skate (n.)
rol•ler-skat•ing
rol•ling
Ro•man **Cath**•o•lic
ro•**mance**
  also pronounced
  ro•mance
Ro•man **nu**•mer•al
ro•**man**•tic
romp
roof
rook
rook•ie
room
room•mate
room•y
roost
roost•er
root
rope
rose
rose•bud
Rosh Ha•**sha**•na
ros•y
rot
ro•ta•ry
ro•tate
ro•tat•ing
ro•**ta**•tion

rote (sounds like
  "wrote")
  *She learned her times
  tables by rote.*
ro•tor
rot•ten
rouge
rough
rough•age
round
round•a•bout
round•house
round•up
route
rou•tine
row (sounds like "roe")
  Row your boat.
row•boat
row•dy
rowed (sounds like
  "road" and "rode")
  I rowed my boat.
roy•al
roy•al•ty
rub
rub•ber
rub•bish
rub•ble
ru•by
rud•der
rude
ruf•fi•an
ruf•fle
rug

rug•by
rug•ged
ru•in
rule
rul•er
rum
rum•ble
rum•mage
rum•mag•ing
ru•mor
rump
rum•ple
run
run•a•way
run-**down**
rung
run•ner
run•ner-**up**
run•ning
run•ny
run•way
ru•ral
rush
rust
rus•tic
rus•tle
rus•tling
rut
ruth•less
rye (sounds like "wry")
  *I made a sandwich
  with rye bread.*

Sab•bath
sa•ber
sa•ber-**toothed ti**•ger
sa•ble
sab•o•tage
sab•o•tag•ing
sab•o•**teur**
sac (sounds like "sack")
 A pouch in an animal's body is a sac.
sac•cha•rin (sounds like "saccharine")
 She put saccharin in her tea.
sac•cha•rine (sounds like "saccharin")
 Her performance as Melanie was saccharine.
sack (sounds like "sac")
 Everything I own is in that sack.
sa•cred
sac•ri•fice
sac•ri•**fi**•cial
sac•ri•fic•ing
sac•ri•lege
sac•ri•le•gious
sad
sad•den
sad•der
sad•dest
sad•dle

sad•dling
sad•ly
sad•ness
sa•**fa**•ri
safe
safe•guard
safe•ty
safe•ty belt
safe•ty pin
sag
sage
sage•brush
sagged
sag•ging
said
sail (sounds like "sale")
 The wind filled the boat's sail.
sail•or
saint
Saint Ber•**nard**
saint•ed
sake
sal•ad
sal•a•man•der
sal•a•ries
sal•a•ry
sale (sounds like "sail")
 They're having a sale on computers.
sales•man
sales•per•son

sales•wom•an
sa•line
sa•**lin**•i•ty
sa•**li**•va
salm•on
sal•mo•**nel**•la
sa•**loon**
sal•sa
salt
salt•wa•ter
sa•**lute**
sa•**lut**•ing
sal•vage
sal•vag•er
sal•vag•ing
sal•**va**•tion
salve
same
sam•ple
sam•pling
sam•u•rai
sanc•tu•aries
sanc•tu•ar•y
sand
san•dal
sand•bag
sand•bar
sand•box
sand•pa•per
sand•pip•er
sand•stone
sand•wich

sand•wich•es
sand•y
sane
san•i•tar•y
san•i•**ta**•tion
san•i•ty
sank
San•ta **Claus**
sap
sap•ling
sapped
sap•phire
sap•ping
sar•casm
sar•**cas**•tic
sar•**dine**
sa•ri
sa•**rong**
sash
Sas•**katch**•e•wan
sat
Sa•tan
satch•el
sat•el•lite
sat•in
sat•ire
sa•**tir**•i•cal
sat•i•rist
sat•is•**fac**•tion
sat•is•**fac**•to•ry
sat•is•fied
sat•is•fies
sat•is•fy
sat•is•fy•ing

sat•u•rate
sat•u•rat•ing
sat•u•**ra**•tion
Sat•ur•day
Sat•urn
sauce
sauce•pan
sau•cer
sau•na
saun•ter
sau•sage
sav•age
sa•**van**•na (or
   sa•**van**•nah)
save
sav•ing
sav•ings
sa•vor•y

saw

saw
saw•dust
saw•mill

sax•o•phone
sax•o•phon•ist
say
say•ing
sa•yo•**na**•ra
scab
scab•bard
scaf•fold
scald
scale
scal•ing
scal•lop
scalp
scal•pel
scam•per
scan
scan•dal
scan•dal•ous
Scan•di•**na**•vi•a
Scan•di•**na**•vi•an
scanned
scan•ner
scan•ning
scape•goat
scar
scarce
scarce•ly
scar•ci•ty
scare
scare•crow
scarf
scar•ing
scar•let
scarves

scat·ter
scat·ter·brained
scav·enge
sce·**nar**·i·o
sce·**nar**·i·os
scene (sounds like "seen")

That was the most exciting scene in the play.

scen·er·y
sce·nic
scent (sounds like "cent" and "sent")

That's a lovely scent you're wearing.

scep·ter
sched·ule
sched·ul·ing
scheme
schem·er
schem·ing
schol·ar
schol·ar·ship
school
school yard
schoon·er
sci·ence
sci·en·**tif**·ic
sci·en·tist
scis·sors
scoff
scold
sco·li·o·sis

scone
scoop
scoot·er
scope
scorch
score
scor·ing
scorn
scorn·ful
scor·pi·on
scour
scour·er
scourge
scout

scowl
scrag·gi·er
scrag·gi·est
scrag·gy
scram·ble
scram·bled
scram·bler

scram·bling
scrap·book
scrape
scraped
scrap·er
scrap·ing
scrapped
scrap·ping
scratch
scratch·i·er
scratch·i·est
scratch·y
scrawl
scream
screech
screen
screw
screw·driv·er
scrib·ble
scrib·bling
scribe
scrim·mage
script
scrip·ture
script·writ·er
scroll
scrounge
scroung·ing
scrub
scrubbed
scrub·bing
scruff·i·er
scruff·i·est
scruff·y

scru•ple
scru•ples
scru•pu•lous
scru•ti•nize
scru•ti•niz•ing
scru•ti•ny
scu•ba
scuff
scuf•fle
scull
sculpt
sculp•tor
sculp•ture
scum
scur•ried
scur•ries
scur•ry
scur•vy
sea (sounds like "see")
The ship was lost at sea.
sea a•**nem**•o•ne
sea•board
sea•far•ing
sea•food
sea•gull
sea horse
seal
sea lev•el
sea li•on
seam (sounds like "seem")
She ripped the seam of her dress.
seam•stress

sea•plane
sea•port
search
search•er
search•ing
search•light
sea•shell
sea•shore
sea•sick
sea•son
sea•son•al
sea•soned
sea•soning
seat
seat belt
sea ur•chin
sea•weed
se•**cede**
se•**ced**•ed
se•**ces**•sion
se•**clud**•ed
se•cond
sec•on•dar•y
sec•ond•hand
sec•ond-**rate**
se•cre•cy
se•cret
sec•re•**tar**•i•al
sec•re•tar•ies
sec•re•tar•y
se•**crete**
se•cre•tive
  also pronounced
  se•**cre**•tive

sec•tion
sec•tor
se•**cure**
se•**cur**•ing
se•**cu**•ri•ties
se•**cu**•ri•ty
se•**dan**
se•**date**
se•**dat**•ing
se•**da**•tion
sed•a•tive
sed•i•ment
sed•i•**men**•tary
sed•i•men•**ta**•tion
see (sounds like "sea")
Can you see the parade from here?
seed
seed•ling
seek
seem (sounds like "seam")
You seem to be in a happy mood today.
seen (sounds like "scene")
The president was seen on television.
seep
see•saw
seethe
seeth•ing
seg•ment
seg•**men**•tal

seg•re•gate

seg•re•gat•ing

seg•re•**ga**•tion

seis•mo•graph

seize

seiz•ing

sei•zure

sel•dom

se•**lect**

se•**lec**•tion

se•**lec**•tive

se•**lec**•tor

self

self-**cen**•tered

self-**con**•fi•dence

self-**con**•fi•dent

self-**con**•scious

self-con•**trol**

self-con•**trolled**

self-de•**fense**

self-de•**struct**

self-de•**struc**•tion

self-de•**struc**•tive

self-em•**ployed**

self-em•**ploy**•ment

self-es•**teem**

self-ex•**plan**•a•tory

self•ish

self•ish•ness

self-re•**spect**

self-re•**spect**•ing

self-**serv**•ice

self-**start**•er

self-suf•**fi**•cien•cy

self-suf•**fi**•cient

sell (sounds like "cell")

Did he sell you his bike?

sel•ler

se•**mes**•ter

sem•i•cir•cle

sem•i•**cir**•cu•lar

sem•i•co•lon

sem•i•con•**duc**•tor

sem•i•fi•nal

sem•i•nar•ies

sem•i•nar•y

Sem•i•nole

sen•ate

sen•a•tor

send

send-off

se•nile

se•**nil**•i•ty

sen•ior

sen•ior **cit**•i•zen

sen•**ior**•i•ty

sen•**sa**•tion

sen•**sa**•tion•al

sense

sense•less

sen•si•ble

sen•si•bly

sens•ing

sen•si•tive

sen•si•**tiv**•i•ty

sen•sor

sent (sounds like "cent" and "scent")

She sent me a birthday present.

sen•tence

sen•ti•ment

sen•ti•**ment**•al

sen•ti•ment•**al**•i•ty

sep•a•rate

sep•a•rat•ing

sep•a•**ra**•tion

Sep•**tem**•ber

se•quel

se•quence

se•**quen**•tial

se•**quoi**•a

ser•en•**dip**•i•tous

ser•en•**dip**•i•ty

se•**rene**

se•**ren**•i•ty

serf (sounds like "surf")

The serf worked on the lord's land.

serf•dom

ser•geant

se•ri•al (sounds like "cereal")

Her book was made into a TV serial.

se•ri•a•li•**za**•tion

se•ri•a•lize

se•ri•al **num**•ber

se•ries

se•ri•ous

se•ri•ous•ness
ser•mon
ser•pent
se•rum
serv•ant
serve
serv•er
serv•ice
serv•ic•ing
ses•a•me
ses•sion
set
set•back
set•**tee**
set•ting
set•tle
set•tle•ment
set•tling
set•up
sev•en
sev•enth
sev•er
sev•er•al
se•**vere**
se•**ver**•i•ty
sew (sounds like "so" and "sow")
I have to sew this button on.
sew•age
sew•er
sew•ing ma•**chine**
sex
sex•ism

sex•ist
shab•bi•ly
shab•by
shack
shade
shad•ing
shad•ow
shag•gi•er
shag•gi•est
shag•gy
shake
shak•en
shak•i•er
shak•i•est
shak•ing
shak•y
shall
shal•low
sham•bles
shame
sham•poo
sham•rock
shape
shape•less
shap•ing
share
share•ware
shar•ing
shark
sharp
shat•ter
shave
shav•ing
shawl

Shaw•**nee**
she
sheaf
shear (sounds like "sheer")
Use these clippers to shear the hedge.
shears
sheath
shed
she'd
sheen
sheep
sheep•dog
sheep•ish
sheer (sounds like "shear")
Mom hung sheer curtains in the kitchen.
sheet

shark

sheik (*or* sheikh)
shelf
shell
she'll
shel•**lac**
shel•ter
shelve
shelves
shelv•ing
shep•herd
sher•bet (*or* sher•bert)
sher•iff
sher•iffs
sher•ry
she's
Shet•land **po**•ny
shied
shield
shi•er (*or* shy•er)
shies
shi•est (*or* shy•est)
shift
shim•mer
shin
shine
shin•gle
shin•gling
shin•ing
shin•ning
Shin•to
shi•ny
ship
ship•ment

shipped
ship•ping
ship•shape
ship•wreck
ship•yard
shirk
shirt
shish ka•bob (*or* shish ke•bob)
shiv•er
shiv•er•y
shoal
shock
shod•di•er
shod•di•est
shod•dy
shoe
shoe•horn
shoe•lace

(ship)

shoes
shone (sounds like "shown")
The sun shone all day.
shook
shoot (sounds like "chute")
They're going to shoot a movie in our house!
shoot•ing **star**
shop
shop•keeper
shop•lift•er
shopped
shop•ping
shop•ping **cen**•ter
shore
short
short•age
short•bread
short **cir**•cuit
short•com•ing
short•en
short•en•ing
short•hand
short•**hand**•ed
short•ly
short-range
short•sight•ed
short•sight•ed•ness
short•stop
short-temp•ered
shot
shot•gun

shot put
should
shoul·der
shoul·der blade
should·n't
should·'ve
shout
shove
shov·el
shov·ing
show
show busi·ness
show·er
show·er·y
shown (sounds like
   "shone")
   *I have shown him
   around.*
show-off
show·room
show·y
shrank
shrap·nel
shred
shred·ded
shred·der
shred·ding
shrewd
shriek
shrill
shrimp
shrine
shrink
shriv·el

shrub
shrub·ber·y
shrug
shrugged
shrug·ging
shrunk
shrunk·en
shud·der
shuf·fle
shuf·fled
shuf·fling
shun
shunned
shun·ning
shut
shut·ter
shut·tle
shut·tling
shy
shy·er (*or* shi·er)
shy·est (*or* shi·est)
shy·ness
Si·a·mese
sib·ling
sick
sick·en
sick·le
sick·le-cell a·ne·mi·a
sick·li·er
sick·li·est
sick·ly
sick·ness
side
side·board

side·burns
sid·ed
side ef·fect
side·line
side·show
side·step
side·stepped
side·step·ping
side·track
side·walk
side·ways
sid·ing
siege
si·er·ra
si·es·ta
sieve
sift
sigh
sighed
sight (sounds like
   "cite" and "site")
   *Niagara Falls is an
   awesome sight.*
sight·se·er
sign
sig·nal
sig·na·ture
sig·nif·i·cance
sig·nif·i·cant
sig·ni·fy
sig·ni·fy·ing
sign lan·guage
sign·post
Sikh

si•lence
si•lenc•er
si•lent
sil•hou•**ette**
sil•i•con
silk
silk•y
sil•li•er
sil•li•est
sil•li•ness
sil•ly
si•lo
silt
sil•ver
sil•ver•smith
sil•ver•ware
sil•ver•y
sim•i•lar
sim•i•**lar**•i•ties
sim•i•**lar**•i•ty
sim•i•le
sim•mer
sim•ple
sim•pler
sim•plest
sim•**plic**•i•ty
sim•pli•fi•**ca**•tion
sim•pli•fied
sim•pli•fies
sim•pli•fy
sim•ply
sim•u•late
sim•u•lat•ing
sim•u•**la**•tion

sim•u•la•tor
si•mul•**ta**•ne•ous
sin
since
sin•**cere**
sin•**cere**•ly
sin•**cer**•i•ty
sing
sin•gle
sin•gle-**hand**•ed
sin•gle-**mind**•ed
sin•gu•lar
sin•i•ster
sink
sinned
sin•ner
sin•ning
si•nus
Sioux (sounds like "sue")
  The Sioux inhabited the northern Great Plains.
sip
sipped
sip•ping
sir
si•ren
sis•ter
sis•ter•hood
sis•ter-in-law
sis•ters-in-law
sit
sit•com

site (sounds like "cite" and "sight")
  This is a perfect site for our house.
sit•ting
sit•u•ate
sit•u•at•ing
sit•u•**a**•tion
sit-up
six
sixth
siz•a•ble (*or* **size**•a•ble)
size
siz•zle
siz•zling
skate
skate•board
skel•e•ton
skep•tic
skep•ti•cal
sketch
sketch•y
skew•er
ski
skid
skid•ded
skid•ding
skied
skies
ski•ing
skill
skilled
skil•let
skill•ful

skim
skim milk
skin
skinned
skin·ni·er
skin·ni·est
skin·ni·ness
skin·ning
skin·ny
skip
skipped
skip·ping
skirt
skit
skit·tish
skull
skunk
sky
sky·box
sky·dive
sky·div·er
sky·div·ing
sky·lark
sky·light
sky·line
sky·rock·et
sky·scrap·er
slab
slack
slain
sla·lom
slam
slammed
slam·ming

sledding

slan·der
slan·der·ous
slang
slant
slap
slap·dash
slapped
slap·ping
slap·stick
slash
slat
slate
slaugh·ter
slave
slav·ing
slay (sounds like "sleigh")
How did David slay Goliath?
sled
sled·ded

sled·ding
sledge·ham·mer
sleek
sleep
sleep·i·er
sleep·i·est
sleep·i·ness
sleep·ing **bag**
sleep·walk·er
sleepy
sleet
sleeve
sleigh (sounds like "slay")
It's snowing, so hitch up the sleigh.
sleight (sounds like "slight")
The tricks involved sleight of hand.
slen·der
slept
sleuth
slew
slice
slic·ing
slick
slid
slide
slid·ing
slight (sounds like "sleight")
There is a slight chance of rain.

slim

slime

slimmed

slim•ming

sling

sling•shot

slip

slipped

slip•per

slip•per•y

slip•ping

slip•shod

slit

slith•er

sliv•er

slo•gan

sloop

slop

slope

slop•ing

slopped

slop•ping

slop•py

slosh

slot

sloth

slouch

slov•en•ly

slow

slow•ly

sludge

slug

slugged

slug•ging

slug•gish

slug•gish•ness

slum

slum•ber

slump

slur

slurp

slurred

slur•ring

slush

sly

smack

small

small•pox

smart

smart•ness

smash

smear

smell

smell•y

smile

smil•ing

smirk

smock

smog

smoke

smoke a•larm

smoke de•tec•tor

smoke•stack

smok•y

smol•der

smooth

smooth•ness

smoth•er

smudge

smudg•ing

smug

smug•gle

snack

snag

snagged

snag•ging

snail

snake

snak•ing

snap

snap•drag•on

snap•shot

snare drum

snatch

sneak

sneak•ers

sneak•i•ly

sneer

smokestack

sneeze

sneez•ing

snick•er

sniff

snif•fle

snip

snipe

snip•er

snip•ing

snipped

snip•ping

snob

snob•ber•y

snoop

snoop•y

snoot•y

snooze

snooz•ing

snore

snor•ing

snor•kel

snort

snout

snow

snow•ball

snow•flake

snow•mo•bile

snow•plow

snow•shoe

snow•storm

snow•y

snub

snubbed

snub•bing

snuff

snuf•fle

snuf•fling

snug

snug•ger

snug•gest

snug•gle

snug•gled

snug•gling

snug•gly
(often confused
with "snugly")
*The teddy bear was
soft and snuggly.*

snug•ly
(often confused
with "snuggly")
The dress fit snugly.

so (sounds like "sew"
and "sow")
*He was so tired after
the race, he fell
asleep.*

soak

soak•ing

soap

soap op•er•a

soar

sob

sobbed

sob•bing

so•ber

soc•cer

so•cia•ble

so•cia•bil•i•ty

so•cia•bly

so•cial

so•cial•ism

so•cial•ly

So•cial Se•cu•ri•ty

so•cial stud•ies

so•ci•e•ties

so•ci•e•ty

so•ci•o•log•i•cal

so•ci•ol•o•gist

so•ci•ol•o•gy

sock

sock•et

sod

so•da

so•da foun•tain

so•da wa•ter

sod•den

sod•ding

so•di•um

so•di•um
bi•car•bon•ate

so•fa

soft

soft•ball

soft drink

soft•heart•ed

soft•ness

soft•ware

sog•gi•er

sog•gi•est

sog•gy

soil

sol•ace

so•lar
so•lar **en**•er•gy
so•lar **sys**•tem
sold
sol•dier
sole (sounds like "soul")
 Tom was the sole
 survivor.
sol•emn
sol•em•ness
sol•id
sol•i•**dar**•i•ty
so•**lid**•i•fy
sol•id•ly
sol•i•tar•y
sol•i•tar•y
 con•**fine**•ment
so•lo
so•loed
so•lo•ing
so•los
sol•u•ble
so•**lu**•tion
solve
sol•vent
solv•er
solv•ing
som•ber
som•**bre**•ro
som•**bre**•ros
some
some•bod•y
some•day
some•how

some•one
som•er•sault
some•thing
some•time
some•times
some•what
some•where
son (sounds like "sun")
 His son left for college
 this fall.
so•nar
so•**na**•ta
song
son•ic
son•ic **boom**
son-in-law
son•net
sons-in-law
soon
soot
soothe
sooth•ing
so•**phis**•ti•ca•ted
so•phis•ti•**ca**•tion
Soph•o•cles
soph•o•more
sop•ping
so•**pran**•o
so•**pran**•os
sor•**bet**
 also pronounced
 sor•bet
sor•cer•er
sor•cer•y

sor•did
sor•did•ness
sore
sore•ness
sor•ri•er
sor•ri•est
sor•row
sor•row•ful
sor•ry
sort
sought
soul (sounds like "sole")
 I love you to the
 bottom of my soul.
sound
sound•proof
soup
sour
source
sour•dough
south
South Car•o•**li**•na
South Da•**ko**•ta
South•**east**
south•ern
South•ern
 Hem•i•sphere
South Pole
South•**west**
sou•ve•**nir**
 also pronounced
 sou•ve•nir
sov•er•eign
So•vi•et **Un**•ion

sow (sounds like "sew" and "so")

The farmer must sow his seeds.

sow (rhymes with "cow")

The sow gave birth to eight piglets.

soy•bean

soy sauce

space

space bar

space•craft

space•ship

space•suit

space•walk

spac•ing

spa•cious

spade

spa•**ghet**•ti

span

spank

spanned

span•ning

spare

spar•ing

spark

spar•kle

spark•ling

spark plug

spar•row

sparse

spas•m

spat

spat•ter

spat•u•la

spawn

speak

speak•er

spear

spear•mint

spe•cial

spe•cial•ist

spe•cial•ize

spe•cial•iz•ing

spe•cial•ties

(spacesuit)

spe•cial•ty

spe•cies

spe•**ci**•fic

spe•**ci**•fi•cal•ly

spe•ci•fi•**ca**•tions

spec•i•fied

spec•i•fies

spec•i•fy

spec•i•fy•ing

spec•i•men

speck

speck•led

spec•ta•cle

spec•**tac**•u•lar

spec•ta•tor

spec•ter

spec•tral

spec•trum

spec•u•late

spec•u•lat•ing

spec•u•**la**•tion

speech

speech•less

speed

speed bump

speed•**om**•e•ter

spell

spell check•er

spe•**lunk**•ing

spend

sperm

sphere

spher•i•cal

sphinx

spice

spi•cy

spi•der

spied

spies

spike
spik•ing
spill
spin
spin•ach
spi•nal
spi•nal **cord**
spin•dle
spind•ly
spine
spin•ning
spin•ning **wheel**
spin-off
spin•ster
spin•y
spi•ral
spire
spir•it
spir•i•tu•al
spit
spite
spit•ting
splash
splash•down
splat•ter
splen•did
splen•dor
splint
splin•ter
split
split•ting
spoil
spoke
spok•en

sponge
spong•y
spon•sor
spon•sor•ship
spon•ta•**ne**•i•ty
spon•**ta**•ne•ous
spool
spoon
spore
sport
sports•man•ship
spot
spot•less
spot•light
spot•ted

spotted

spot•ting
spouse
spout
sprain
sprang
sprawl

spray
spread
spree
spring
spring•board
spring-
clean•ing
spring•time
sprin•kle
sprin•kler
sprink•ling
sprint
sprout
spruce
sprung
spun
spur
spurt
sput•ter
spy
spy•ing
squab•ble
squab•bling
squad
squad•ron
squan•der
square
square dance
square root
squash
squat•ter
squawk
squeak
squeal

squea·mish

squeez·a·ble

squeeze

squeez·ing

squid

squig·gle

squinch

squint

squire

squirm

squir·rel

squirt

squish·y

stab

stabbed

stab·bing

sta·bi·lize

sta·ble

stac·**ca**·to

stack

sta·di·um

staff

stag

stage

stage·coach

stag·ger

stag·ger·ing

stag·ing

stag·nant

stag·**na**·tion

staid

stain

stained glass

stain·less **steel**

---

stair (sounds like "stare")

She tripped on the stair and fell.

stair·way

stake (sounds like "steak")

Use this stake to set up the tent.

stak·ing

sta·**lac**·tite

sta·**lag**·mite

stale

stale·mate

stalk

stall

stal·lion

sta·men

stam·i·na

stam·mer

stamp

stam·**pede**

stam·**ped**·ing

stand

stan·dard

stand·by

stand-in

stand·ing

stand·still

stand-up

stank

stan·za

sta·ple

star

---

star·board

starch

star·dom

star·dust

stare (sounds like "stair")

You shouldn't stare at people.

stared

star·fish

star·gaz·er

star·ing

stark

star·less

star·light

star·ling

star·ry-eyed

star-spang·led

star-stud·ded

start

star·tle

start·ling

star·**va**·tion

starve

starv·ing

state

state·ly

state·ment

state-of-the-art

stat·ic

stat·ic e·lec·**tric**·i·ty

stat·ing

sta·tion

sta•tion•ar•y (sounds
   like "stationery")
   *The stationary target
   was easy to hit.*
sta•tion•er•y (sounds
   like "stationary")
   *I'll buy envelopes at
   the stationery store.*
sta•tion **wag**•on
sta•**tis**•tic
sta•tus
stay
stead•fast
stead•i•ly
stead•y
steak (sounds like
   "stake")
   He likes to eat steak.
steal (sounds like
   "steel")
   *Did your brother steal
   your wallet?*
stealth
stealth•y
steam
steam•boat
steam en•gine
steam•rol•ler
steam•ship
steed
steel (sounds like
   "steal")
   *The bridge is made
   of steel.*
steel wool

steep
stee•ple
steer
steer•ing
steg•o•**sau**•rus
stel•lar
stem
stemmed
stem•ming
stench
sten•cil
step (sounds like
   "steppe")
   *Step right up, ladies
   and gentlemen.*
step•fami•lies
step•fami•ly
step•fa•ther
step•moth•er
steppe (sounds like
   "step")
   *A steppe is a vast,
   grassy plain.*
stepped
step•ping
ste•re•o
ste•r•eos
ster•e•o•type
ster•ile
ster•il•i•**za**•tion
ster•i•lize
ster•ling
stern
ste•roid

steth•o•scope
stew
stew•ard
stew•ard•ess
stick
stick•er
sties (*or* **styes**)
stiff
stif•fen
sti•fle
sti•fling
stig•ma
stig•ma•tize
still
stilt
stim•u•lant
stim•u•late
stim•u•lat•ing
stim•u•**la**•tion
stim•u•lus
sting
sting•er
sting•ray
stin•gy
stink
stir
stir-fried
stir-fries
stir-fry
stirred
stir•ring
stir•rup
stitch
stock

stock•**ade**
stock•bro•ker
stock car
stock•hold•er
Stock•holm
stock•ing
stock•pile
stocks
stock•y
stock•yard
stodg•i•er
stodg•i•est
stodg•y
sto•ic
stoke
stok•ing
stole
sto•len
stom•ach
stom•ach•ache
stomp
stone
stone•wall
stone•washed
stood
stool
stoop
stop
stop•light
stopped
stop•per
stop•ping
stop•watch
stor•age

store
store•keep•er
sto•ries
stor•ing
stork

stork

storm
sto•ry
stout
stove
stow
stow•a•way
strag•**gle**
strag•gler
strag•gling
straight (sounds like "strait")

She rushed straight home after work.

straight•en

strain
strait (sounds like "straight")

We sailed quickly through the strait.

strand
strange
strange•ly
strange•ness
strang•er
strang•est
stran•gle
stran•gler
stran•gling
stran•gu•**la•**tion
strap
strapped
strap•ping
strat•e•gies
strat•e•gist
strat•e•gy
strat•o•sphere
straw
straw•ber•ries
straw•ber•ry
stray
streak
streak•y
stream
stream•er
stream•lined
street
street•light
street•wise

strength
strength•en
stren•u•ous
stress
stress•ful
stretch
strict
stride
strid•ing
strife
strike
strik•er
strik•ing
string
string bean
strings
strip
stripped
strip•ping
stripe
strive
striv•en
striv•ing
strobe
stroke
stroll
strong
strong•hold
struc•ture
strug•gle
strug•gling
strum
strummed
strut

strut•ted
stub
stubbed
stub•bing
stub•born
stuck
stuck-up
stu•dent
stud•ied
stud•ies
stu•di•o
stu•di•os
stu•di•ous
stud•y
stud•y•ing
stuff
stuf•fing
stuf•fy
stum•ble
stum•bling
stump
stump•y
stun
stunk
stunned
stun•ning
stunt
stu•pen•dous
stu•pid
stu•pid•i•ty
stur•dy
stut•ter
stut•ter•er
sty

styes (or sties)
style
sty•ling
sty•lish
sty•list
Sty•ro•foam
sub•con•scious
sub•con•ti•nent
sub•di•vide
   also pronounced
   sub•di•vide
sub•di•vi•sion
   also pronounced
   sub•di•vi•sion
sub•ject (n.)
sub•ject (v.)
sub•ma•rine
   also pronounced
   sub•ma•rine
sub•merge
sub•mit
sub•mit•ted
sub•mit•ting
sub•scribe
sub•scrib•er
sub•scrib•ing
sub•scrip•tion
sub•se•quent
sub•set
sub•si•dies
sub•si•dize
sub•si•dy
sub•stance
sub•stan•tial

sub•sti•tute
sub•sti•**tu**•tion
sub•ter•**ra**•ne•an
sub•ti•tle
sub•tle
sub•tle•ty
sub•**tract**
sub•**trac**•tion
sub•tra•hend
sub•**trop**•ics
sub•urb
sub•**ur**•ban
sub•**ur**•ban•ite
sub•**ur**•bi•a
sub•way
suc•**ceed**
suc•**cess**
suc•**cess**•ful
suc•cu•lent
such
suck
suck•er
suc•tion
sud•den
sud•den•ness
suds
sue (sounds like
  "Sioux")
  *She's going to sue
  him in court.*
suede
suf•fer
suf•**fi**•cient
suf•fix

suf•fo•cate
suf•fo•cat•ing
suf•fo•**ca**•tion
suf•frage
sug•ar

sugar

sug•ar•y
sug•**gest**
sug•**gest**•ion
su•i•**ci**•dal
su•i•cide
su•ing
suit
suit•a•**bil**•i•ty
suit•a•ble
suit•a•bly
suit•case
suite (sounds like
  "sweet")
  *We had a big suite at
  the hotel.*

sul•fur
sul•fur di•**ox**•ide
sulk
sulk•y
sul•len
sul•tan
sul•try
sum
su•mac
sum•ma•ries
sum•ma•rize
sum•ma•ry (sounds
  like "summery")
  *Write a summary of
  the book.*
sum•**ma**•tion
summed
sum•mer
sum•mer•time
sum•mer•y (sounds
  like "summary")
  *It was a warm,
  summery day.*
sum•ming
sum•mit
sum•mon
sum•mons
su•mo **wres**•tling
sun (sounds like "son")
  *The sun is over
  90 million miles from
  Earth.*
sun•bath (n.)
sun•bathe (v.)

sun·burn
sun·dae (sounds like "Sunday")
Have an ice-cream sundae.
Sun·day (sounds like "sundae")
Sunday comes before Monday.
sun·dial
sun·down
sun·flow·er
sun·glass·es
sunk
sunk·en
sun·light
sun·ny
sun·rise
sun·screen
sun·set
sun·shine
sun·stroke
sun·tan
su·per
su·perb
su·per·fi·cial
su·per·her·o
su·per·hu·man
su·per·im·pose
su·per·in·ten·dent
su·pe·ri·or
su·pe·ri·or·i·ty
su·per·la·tive
su·per·mar·ket

su·per·nat·u·ral
su·per·no·va
su·per·pow·er
su·per·son·ic
su·per·sti·tion
su·per·sti·tious
su·per·tank·er
su·per·vise
su·per·vis·ing
su·per·vi·sion
su·per·vi·sor
sup·per
sup·ple
sup·ple·ment
sup·ple·men·ta·ry
sup·plied
sup·pli·er
sup·plies
sup·ply
sup·ply·ing
sup·port
sup·port·er
sup·port·ive
sup·pose
su·preme
sure
sure·ly
surf (sounds like "serf")
Surf's up!
sur·face
sur·fac·ing
surf·board
surf·er
surge

sur·geon
sur·ger·y
sur·gi·cal
sur·li·ness
sur·ly
sur·pass
sur·plus
sur·prise
sur·pris·ing
sur·ren·der
sur·round
sur·round·ings
sur·vey (v.)
sur·vey (n.)
sur·viv·al
sur·vive
sur·viv·ing
sur·vi·vor
sus·pect (v.)
sus·pect (n.)
sus·pend
sus·pend·ers
sus·pense
sus·pen·sion
sus·pi·cion
sus·pi·cious
swag·ger
swal·low
swam
swamp
swamp·y
swan
swap
swapped

swap·ping

swarm

swarth·y

swas·ti·ka

swat

swat·ted

swat·ting

sway

swear

sweat

sweat·er

sweat·shirt

sweep

sweep·ing

sweet (sounds like "suite")

This candy is sweet.

sweet·en

sweet·heart

swell

swel·ter

swel·ter·ing

swept

swerve

swerv·ing

swift

swift·ness

swig

swigged

swig·ging

swim

swim·mer

swim·ming

swim·suit

swin·dle

swin·dler

swin·dling

swine

swing

swipe

swip·ing

swirl

swish

switch

switch·board

swiv·el

swol·len

swoon

swoop

sword

sword·fish

swore

sworn

swum

swung

swelter

syc·a·more

syl·la·ble

syl·la·bus

sym·bol (sounds like "cymbal")

The Statue of Liberty is a symbol of freedom.

sym·bol·ize

sym·**met**·ri·cal

sym·me·try

sym·pa·thize

sym·pa·thy

sym·**phon**·ic

sym·pho·nies

sym·pho·ny

symp·tom

syn·a·gogue

syn·chro·nize

syn·co·pate

syn·drome

syn·o·nym

syn·**op**·ses (pl.)

syn·**op**·sis (sing.)

syn·the·size

syn·the·siz·er

syn·**thet**·ic

sy·phon

Syr·i·a

sy·**ringe**

syr·up

sys·tem

sys·tem·**at**·ic

sys·tem·**at**·i·cal·ly

tab
tabbed
tab•bing
tab•by
tab•er•na•cle
ta•ble
ta•ble•cloth
ta•ble•spoon
tab•let
ta•ble **ten**•nis
tab•loid
ta•**boo**
tab•u•late
tab•u•lat•ing
tab•u•**la**•tion
tack
tack•le
ta•co
ta•cos
tact
tact•ful
tac•ti•cal
tac•tics
tad•pole
taf•fy
tag
tagged
tag•ging
tail (sounds like "tale")
  *The dog wags its tail
  when it's happy.*
tail•gate

tail•gat•ing
tai•lor
take
take•off
take•out

(**tambourine**)

take•o•ver
tak•ing
tal•cum **pow**•der
tale (sounds like "tail")
  *He told me an exciting
  tale of adventure.*
tal•ent
talk
talk•a•tive
tall
tal•lied
tal•lies
tal•ly
Tal•mud

tal•on
ta•**ma**•le
tam•bou•**rine**
tame
tam•per
tan
tan•dem
tan•**door**•i
tan•ge•lo
tan•gent
tan•ger•**ine**
tan•gle
tan•gling
tan•gram
tang•y
tank
tank•er
tanned
tan•ner•y
tan•ning
tan•trum
tap
tap danc•ing
tape
taped
tape meas•ure
ta•per
tape re•**cord**•er
tap•es•try
tap•ing
tapped
tap•ping

taps
tar
ta•**ran**•tu•la
tar•di•ness
tar•dy
tar•get
tar•iff
tar•nish
tar•pau•lin
tarred
tar•ring
tart
tar•tan
tar•tar
task
tas•sel
taste
taste bud
taste•less
tast•ing
tat•tered
tat•tle
tat•tler
tat•tle•tale
tat•tling
tat•too
taught
taunt
tav•ern
tax
tax•**a**•tion
tax•i
tax•i•cab
tax•ied

tax•ies (v.)
tax•i•ing
tax•is (pl. n.)
tea
teach
teach•er
tea•ket•tle
teal
team (sounds like "teem")
I made the football team!
team•mate
tear (sounds like "tier")
I cried many a tear.
tear (rhymes with "hare")
Don't tear the magazine.
tease
teased
teas•ing
tea•spoon
tea•spoon•ful
tech•ni•cal
tech•**ni**•cian
tech•**nique**
tech•no•**log**•i•cal
tech•**nol**•o•gies
tech•**nol**•o•gy
ted•dy **bear**
te•di•ous
teem (sounds like "team")

The city streets teem with people.
teen•age (*or* **teen**-age)
teen•aged (*or* **teen**-aged)
teen•ag•er (*or* **teen**-ag•er)
teens
tee•pee (*or* **te**•pee)
tee shirt (*or* **T**-shirt)
teeth
teethe
teeth•ing
Tef•lon
tel•e•cast
tel•e•com•mu•ni•**ca**•tion
tel•e•com•**mute**
tel•e•com•**mut**•er
tel•e•com•**mut**•ing
tel•e•gram
tel•e•graph
tel•e•graph•er
tel•e•mar•ket•ing
tel•e•phone
tel•e•phon•ing
tel•e•**pho**•to **lens**
tel•e•scope
tel•e•**scop**•ic
tel•e•thon
tel•e•vise
tel•e•vis•ing
tel•e•vi•sion
tell

tel•ler
tem•per
tem•per•a•ment
tem•per•a•**men**•tal
tem•per•ate
tem•per•a•ture
tem•pest
tem•plate
tem•ple
tem•po
tem•po•**rar**•i•ly
tem•po•rar•y
tem•pos
tempt
temp•**ta**•tion
tempt•er
ten
ten•ant
tend
ten•den•cies
ten•den•cy
ten•der
ten•der•ness
ten•don
ten•e•ment
Ten•nes•**see**
  also pronounced
  Ten•nes•see
ten•nis
ten•or
tense (sounds like
  "tents")
  Try not to get tense.
ten•sion

tent
ten•ta•cle
ten•ta•tive
ten•ter•hooks
tenth
tents (sounds like
  "tense")
  *How many tents
  were in the camp?*
ten•u•ous
te•pee (*or* **tee**•pee)
tep•id
ter•i•**ya**•ki
term
ter•mi•nal
ter•mi•nate
ter•mi•nat•ing
ter•mite
ter•race
ter•ra-**cot**•ta
ter•**rain**
ter•ra•pin
ter•**rar**•i•um
ter•**res**•tri•al
ter•ri•ble
ter•ri•bly
ter•ri•er
ter•**ri**•fic
ter•ri•fied
ter•ri•fies
ter•ri•fy
ter•ri•fy•ing
ter•ri•**to**•ri•al
ter•ri•to•ries

ter•ri•to•ry
ter•ror
ter•ror•ist
ter•ror•ize
ter•ror•iz•ing
terse
test
tes•ta•ment
test•i•fied
test•i•fies
test•i•fy
test•i•fy•ing
tes•ti•mo•ny
test tube
tet•a•nus
teth•er
Tex•as
Tex-Mex
text
text•book
tex•tile
tex•ture
than
thank
thank•ful
thank•less
Thanks•**giv**•ing **Day**
that
thatch
that's
thaw
the
the•a•ter (*or* **the**•a•tre)
the•**at**•ri•cal

thee

theft

their (sounds like
  "there" and "they're")
  This is their house.

theirs

them

theme

them•**selves**

then

the•o•**log**•i•cal

the•**ol**•o•gy

the•o•rem

the•o•**ret**•i•cal

the•o•ries

the•o•ry

ther•a•pies

ther•a•pist

ther•a•py

there (sounds like
  "their" and "they're")
  *There are the books I
  was looking for.*

there•**af**•ter

there•by
  also pronounced
  there•**by**

there•fore

there's

therm

ther•mal

ther•**mom**•e•ter

ther•mos **bot**•tle

ther•mo•stat

the•**sau**•rus

these

they

they'd

they'll

they're (sounds like
  "their" and "there")
  *They're coming here
  on Sunday.*

they've

thick

(thief)

thief

thieves

thigh

thim•ble

thin

thing

think

thin•ness

third

thirst

thirst•i•er

thirst•i•est

thirst•y

this

this•tle

thong

tho•rax

thorn

thorn•i•er

thorn•i•est

thorn•y

thor•ough

thor•ough•fare

thor•ough•ness

those

thou

though

thought

thought•ful

thought•less

thou•sand

thou•sandth

thrash

thread

thread•bare

threat

threat•en

three

three-di•**men**•sion•al

thresh

thresh•old

threw (sounds like
  "through")
  *She threw the ball
  to the catcher.*

thrift•i•er

thrift•i•est

thrift•i•ness

thrift•y

thrill

thril•ler

thril•ling

thrive

thriv•ing

throat

throb

throne (sounds like "thrown")

The dizzy king fell off his throne.

throng

throt•tle

throt•tling

through (sounds like "threw")

The ball flew right through the window.

through•out

through•way (*or* thru•way)

throw

thrown (sounds like "throne")

My homework was thrown away!

thud

thug

thumb

thumb•tack

thump

thun•der

thun•der•storm

Thurs•day

thus

thwart

thy

thyme (sounds like "time")

Season the food with a little thyme.

ti•ar•a

tick

tick•et

tick•le

tick•ling

tick•lish

tick-tack-toe (*or* tic-tac-toe)

tid•al

tid•al wave

tid•bit

tid•dle•dy•winks (*or* tid•dly•winks)

tide

ti•di•er

ti•di•est

ti•di•ness

tid•ings

ti•dy

tie

tie•break•er

tied

tier (sounds like "tear")

Our theater seats were in the first tier.

ties

ti•ger

(tiger)

ti•ger li•ly

tight

tight•rope

tights

tile

till

till•er

tilt

tim•ber

tim•ber•line

time (sounds like "thyme")

What time does the show begin?

time•keep•er

time•less

time•ly

time-out

time·piece
time·sav·er
time·ta·ble
time·worn
time zone
tim·id
ti·mid·i·ty
tim·id·ness
tin
tinge
tin·gle
tin·gling
ti·ni·er
ti·ni·est
ti·ni·ness
tin·ker
tin·kle
tin·kling
tint
ti·ny
tip
tipped
tip·ping
tip·toe
tire
tired·ness
tire·less
tire·some
tir·ing
tis·sue
ti·tle
Tlin·git
to (sounds like "too"
 and "two")

I'm going to the store.
toad (sounds like
 "towed")
*She caught a toad
in the pond.*
toad·stool
toast
toast·er
to·bac·co
to·bog·gan
to·day
tod·dle
tod·dler
toe (sounds like "tow")
 *What color did you
 paint your big toe?*
tof·fee
to·fu
to·ga
to·geth·er
toil
toil·er
toi·let
to·ken
told
tol·er·ance
tol·er·ant
tol·er·ate
tol·er·at·ing
tol·er·a·tion
toll
tom·a·hawk
to·ma·to
to·ma·toes

tomb
tom·boy
tomb·stone
tom·cat
to·mor·row
ton
tone
tongs
tongue
tongue twist·er
ton·ic
to·night
ton·sil·li·tis
ton·sils
too (sounds like "to"
 and "two")
 It's too hot to dance.
took
tool
tool·box
toot
tooth
tooth·ache
tooth·brush
tooth·paste
tooth·pick
top
to·paz
top·ic
top·i·cal
top·o·graph·i·cal
to·pog·ra·phy
topped
top·ping

top•ple
top•pling
top•soil
top•sy-**tur**•vy
To•rah
torch
to•re•a•dor
tor•ment (n.)
tor•**ment** (v.)
tor•**men**•tor
tor•**na**•do
tor•**na**•does (or
  tor•**na**•dos)
tor•**pe**•do
tor•**pe**•does
tor•rent
tor•rid
tor•so
tor•**til**•la
tor•toise
tor•ture
tor•tur•ing
toss
tot
to•tal
tote
to•tem **pole**
tot•ing
tot•ter
tou•can
touch
touch•down
touch•i•er
touch•i•est

touch•ing
touch•y
tough
tou•**pee**
tour
tour•ism
tour•ist
tour•na•ment
tour•ni•quet
tout
tow (sounds like "toe")
*The tow truck took
my car away.*
toward
  also pronounced
  to•**ward**
towards
  also pronounced
  to•**wards**
towed (sounds like
  "toad")
*My car was towed to
the garage.*
tow•el
tow•er
town
tox•ic
toy
trace
trac•ing
track
tract
trac•tion
trac•tor

trade
trad•ed
trade•mark
trad•er
trad•ing
trad•ing **post**
tra•**di**•tion
traf•fic
traf•ficked
traf•ficking
traf•fic **light**
trag•e•dies
trag•e•dy
trag•ic
trail
trail bike
trail•er
train
train•er
trait
trai•tor
tramp
tram•ple
tram•pling
tram•po•**line**
  also pronounced
  tram•po•line
trance
tran•quil
tran•**quil**•i•ty
tran•quil•ly
trans•**ac**•tion
trans•at•**lan**•tic
trans•con•ti•**nen**•tal

tran•**scribe**
tran•**scrib**•ing
tran•script
tran•**scrip**•tion
trans•**fer**
trans•ferred
trans•**fer**•ring
trans•**form**
trans•for•**ma**•tion
trans•**form**•er
trans•**fu**•sion
tran•sient
tran•**sis**•tor
tran•sit
tran•**si**•tion
tran•si•tive
trans•**late**
  also pronounced
  trans•late
trans•lat•ing
trans•**la**•tion
trans•la•tor
trans•**lu**•cent
trans•**mis**•sion
trans•**mit**
trans•**mit**•ted
trans•**mit**•ter
trans•**mit**•ting
tran•som
trans•**par**•en•cies
trans•**par**•en•cy
trans•**par**•ent
tran•spi•**ra**•tion
tran•**spire**

tran•**spir**•ing
trans•**plant** (v.)
trans•plant (n.)
trans•**port** (v.)
trans•port (n.)
trans•por•**ta**•tion
trap
trap•**door**
tra•**peze**
trap•e•zoid
trapped
trap•per
trap•ping
trash
trau•ma
trau•**mat**•ic
trav•el
trav•el a•gent
trav•el•er
trawl
trawl•er
tray
treach•er•ous
treach•er•y
tread
tread•mill
trea•son
treas•ure
treas•ur•er
treas•u•ry
treat
trea•ties
trea•ty
treb•le

tree
trek
trekked
trek•king
trel•lis
trem•ble
trem•bling
tre•**men**•dous
trem•or
trench
trend
trend•y
tres•pass
tres•pass•er
tres•tle
tri•al

treadmill

tri•an•gle
tri•**an**•gu•lar
tri•**ath**•lon
tri•bal

tribe
trib•u•**la**•tion
tri•**bu**•nal
trib•u•tar•ies
trib•u•tar•y
trib•ute
tri•**ce**•ra•tops
trich•i•**no**•sis
trick
trick•i•er
trick•i•est
trick•i•ness
trick•le
trick•ling
trick or treat (n.)
trick-or-treat (v.)
trick•y
tri•cy•cle
tried
tries
tri•fle
tri•fling
trig•ger
tril•o•gy
trim
trim•ming
trim•mings
tri•o
trip
trip•le
trip•let
tri•pling
tri•pod
tripped

trip•ping
tri•umph
tri•**um**•phant
triv•i•a
triv•i•al
troll
trol•ley
trom•**bone**
troop

trick or treat

troop•er
tro•phies
tro•phy
trop•i•cal
trop•ics
trot
trot•ted
trot•ter

trot•ting
trou•ble
trou•ble•some
trough
trou•sers
trout
tru•an•cy
tru•ant
truce
truck
trudge
trudg•ing
true
tru•ly
trum•pet
trunk
trust
trust•wor•thy
trust•y
truth
truth•ful
try
try•ing
tsar (or **czar**)
tsa•**ri**•na (or cza•**ri**•na)
T-shirt (or **tee** shirt)
tsu•**na**•mi
tub
tu•ba
tube
tu•ber•cu•**lo**•sis
tub•ing
tu•bu•lar
tuck

Tues•day

tug

tugged

tug•ging

tug-of-war

tu•**i**•tion

tu•lip

tum•ble

tum•bler

tum•ble•weed

tum•bling

tum•mies

tum•my

tu•mor

tu•mult

tu•na

tun•dra

tune

tu•nic

tun•ing **fork**

tun•nel

tun•nel **vi**•sion

tur•ban

tur•bine

tur•bo•fan

tur•bu•lent

turf

tur•key

tur•moil

turn

tur•nip

turn•out

turn•pike

turn•stile

turn•ta•ble

tur•pen•tine

tur•quoise

tur•ret

tur•tle

tur•tle•neck

tusk

tus•sle

tus•sling

tu•tor

tu•tu

tux•**e**•do

tux•**e**•dos

tweed

twee•zers

twelfth

twelve

twen•ti•eth

twen•ty

twice

twig

twi•light

twin

twine

twinge

twin•kle

twin•kling

twirl

twist

twis•ter

twitch

twit•ter

two (sounds like "to" and "too")

I'll have two pizzas please.

ty•**coon**

ty•ing

type

type•set

type•set•ter

type•set•ting

type•writ•er

ty•phoid

ty•**phoon**

typ•i•cal

typ•ist

ty•**ran**•ni•cal

ty•**ran**•no•saur

tyr•an•ny

ty•rant

ug•li•er
ug•li•est
ug•ly
u•ku•**le**•le
ul•cer
ul•ti•mate
ul•ti•**ma**•tum
ul•tra
ul•tra•light
ul•tra•**son**•ic
ul•tra•sound
ul•tra•**vi**•o•let
U•**lys**•ses
um•**bil**•i•cal **cord**
um•**brel**•la
um•pire
un•**a**•ble
un•ac•**cept**•a•ble
un•ac•**cus**•tomed
un•af•**fect**•ed
un•**aid**•ed
u•**nan**•i•mous
un•ap•**proach**•a•ble
un•**armed**
un•**au**•tho•rized
un•a•**void**•a•ble
un•a•**void**•a•bly
un•a•**ware**
un•**bear**•a•ble
un•**bear**•a•bly
un•**bẽat**•en
un•be•**com**•ing

un•be•**liev**•a•ble
un•be•**liev**•a•bly
un•**bend**•ing
un•**bi**•ased
un•**break**•a•ble
un•**bro**•ken
un•**bur**•den
un•**but**•ton
un•**can**•ni•ly
un•**can**•ny
un•**cer**•tain
un•**cer**•tain•ty
un•**civ**•i•lized
un•cle
un•**com**•fort•a•ble
un•**com**•fort•a•bly
un•**com**•mon
un•**com**•pro•mis•ing
un•con•**cerned**
un•con•**di**•tion•al
un•con•**firmed**
un•**con**•scious
un•con•sti•**tu**•tion•al
un•con•**trol**•la•ble
un•co•**op**•er•a•tive
un•**couth**
un•**cov**•er
un•**daunt**•ed
un•de•**cid**•ed
un•de•**ni**•able
un•de•**ni**•a•bly
un•der

un•der•arm
un•der•brush
un•der•clothes
un•der•de•**vel**•oped
un•der•dog
un•der•**es**•ti•mate
un•der•**foot**
un•der•**go**
un•der•**goes**
un•der•**gone**
un•der•ground
Un•der•ground
  Rail•road
un•der•hand
un•der•hand•ed
un•der•line
un•der•lin•ing
un•der•mine
un•der•min•ing
un•der•**neath**
un•der•pants
un•der•pass
un•der•**pop**•u•la•ted
un•der•**priv**•i•leged
un•der•**sea**
un•der•shirt
un•der•**stand**
un•der•**stand**•a•ble
un•der•**stand**•a•bly
un•der•**stand**•ing
un•der•**stood**
un•der•**take**

un•der•tak•er
un•der•**took**
un•der•tow
un•der•wa•ter
un•der•wear
un•der•weight
un•der•**went**
un•der•world
un•de•**sir**•a•ble
un•dis•**turbed**
un•**do**
un•**done**
un•**dress**
un•**dy**•ing
un•**earth**
un•**eas**•i•ly
un•**eas**•i•ness
un•**eas**•y
un•em•**ployed**
un•em•**ploy**•ment
un•**e**•qual
un•**e**•ven
un•**e**•vent•ful
un•ex•**pect**•ed
un•**fair**
un•**fair**•ly
un•**fair**•ness
un•**faith**•ful
un•fa•**mil**•iar
un•**fas**•ten
un•**feel**•ing
un•**fin**•ish•ed
un•**fit**
un•**fold**

un•fore•**seen**
un•for•**get**•ta•ble
un•for•**giv**•a•ble
un•**for**•tu•nate
un•**for**•tu•nate•ly
un•**friend**•ly
un•**grate**•ful
un•**hap**•pi•er
un•**hap**•pi•est
un•**hap**•pi•ly
un•**hap**•pi•ness
un•**hap**•py
un•**health**•y
un•**heard**-of
u•ni•corn
u•ni•cy•cle

unicycle

un•i•den•ti•**fi**•a•ble
un•i•**den**•ti•fied
u•ni•form
u•ni•formed

u•ni•**form**•i•ty
u•ni•fi•**ca**•tion
u•ni•fied
u•ni•fies
u•ni•fy
un•im•**por**•tance
un•im•**por**•tant
un•in•**hab**•it•a•ble
un•in•**hab**•it•ed
un•in•**tel**•li•gi•ble
un•in•**ten**•tion•al
un•**in**•ter•est•ed
un•ion
u•**nique**
u•ni•sex
u•ni•son
u•nit
u•**nite**
u•nity
u•ni•**ver**•sal
u•ni•verse
u•ni•**ver**•si•ties
u•ni•**ver**•si•ty
un•**just**
un•**kind**
un•**known**
un•**less**
un•**like**
un•**like**•ly
un•**lim**•it•ed
un•**load**
un•**lock**
un•**luck**•y
un•mis•**tak**•a•ble

un•mis•**tak**•a•bly
un•**nat**•u•ral
un•nec•es•**sar**•i•ly
un•**nec**•es•sar•y
un•ob•**served**
un•**oc**•cu•pied
un•of•**fi**•cial
un•**pack**
un•**pleas**•ant
un•**pleas**•ant•ly
un•**plug**
un•**pop**•u•lar
un•pre•**dict**•a•ble
un•pre•**pared**
un•pro•**voked**
un•**pub**•lish•ed
un•**rav**•el
un•**rea**•son•a•ble
un•rec•og•**niz**•a•ble
un•re•**li**•able
un•**rest**
un•re•**strict**•ed
un•**ri**•valed
un•**roll**
un•**ruf**•fled
un•**rul**•y
un•sat•is•**fac**•to•ry
un•sci•en•**tif**•ic
un•**scru**•pu•lous
un•**seen**
un•**set**•tle
un•**set**•tled
un•**sight**•ly
un•**skilled**

un•**soc**•ia•ble
un•**sound**
un•**speak**•able
un•**sta**•ble
un•**stead**•y
un•suc•**cess**•ful
un•**suit**•a•ble
un•**sure**
un•**tan**•gle
un•**tan**•gling
un•**think**•a•ble
un•**ti**•di•ness
un•**ti**•di•ly
un•**ti**•dy
un•**tie**
un•**tied**

untied

un•**til**
un•**time**•li•ness
un•**time**•ly
un•to
un•**told**
un•**touched**

un•**true**
un•**ty**•ing
un•**used**
un•**u**•su•al
un•**wel**•come
un•**wield**•y
un•**will**•ing
un•**wind**
un•**wor**•thi•ly
un•**wor**•thy
un•**wound**
un•**wrap**
un•**wrapped**
un•**wrap**•ping
up
up•beat
up•bring•ing
up•**date** (v.)
up•**date** (n.)
up•**grade** (or
  up•grade) (v.)
up•grade (n.)
up•grad•ing
up•**heav**•al
up•**held**
up•hill
up•**hold**
up•**hol**•ster
up•**hol**•ster•er
up•**hol**•ster•y
up•keep
up•**on**
up•per
up•per•case

up•per **hand**
up•per•most
up•right
up•ris•ing
up•roar
up•**roar**•i•ous
up•**root**
up•**set** (v.)
up•set (n.)
up•**set**•ting
up•side **down**
up•**stairs**
up•**stream**
up•**tight**
up-to-date
up•ward
ur•**a**•ni•um

Ur•a•nus
  also pronounced
  Ur•**a**•nus
ur•ban
urge
ur•gen•cy
ur•gent
urg•ing
u•rin•ar•y **sys**•tem
u•ri•nate
u•rine
urn (sounds like
  "earn")
  *We saw a large Greek
  urn in the museum.*
us
us•age

use
used
use•ful
use•ful•ness
use•less
us•er-**friend**•ly
ush•er
us•ing
u•su•al
U•tah
u•**ten**•sil
u•ter•us
u•**til**•i•ties
u•**til**•i•ty
u•ti•lize
ut•most
U-turn

va•can•cy
va•cant
va•**ca**•tion
vac•ci•nate
vac•ci•**na**•tion
vac•**cine**
vac•u•um
vague
vain (sounds like "vane" and "vein")
Vain people always think about themselves.
val•e•dic•**to**•ri•an
val•en•tine
Val•en•tine's **Day**
val•iant
val•id
val•i•date
va•**lid**•i•ty
val•ley
val•or
val•u•a•ble
val•u•a•bles
val•ue
val•ues
valve
vam•pire
van
van•dal
van•dal•ism
van•dal•ize

vane (sounds like "vain" and "vein")
The weather vane shows which way the wind blows.
va•**nil**•la
van•ish
van•i•ty
va•**por**
var•i•a•ble
var•i•ant
var•i•**a**•tion
var•ied
var•ies
va•**ri**•e•ties
va•**ri**•e•ty
var•i•ous
var•nish
var•y (sounds like "very")
Apples vary in size.
vase
vas•sal
vast
vast•ness
vat
vault
VCR
veal
veer
veg•an
veg•e•ta•ble

veg•e•**tar**•i•an
veg•e•**ta**•tion
ve•hi•cle
veil
vein (sounds like "vane" and "vain")
This vein carries blood to the heart.
Vel•cro
ve•**loc**•i•ty
vel•vet
ven•**det**•ta
vend•ing
ven•dor
ve•**ne**•tian **blind**
Ven•e•**zue**•la
ven•geance
Ven•ice
ven•i•son
ven•om
ven•om•ous
vent
ven•ti•late
ven•ti•**la**•tion
ven•ti•la•tor
ven•tri•cle
ven•**tril**•o•quist
ven•ture
ven•ture•some
ven•tur•ing
ven•ue
Ve•nus

ve•**ran**•da (*or*
   ve•**ran**•dah)
verb
ver•bal
ver•dict
Ver•gil (*or* **Vir**•gil)
ver•i•fi•**ca**•tion
ver•i•fied
ver•i•fies
ver•i•fy
Ver•**mont**
Ver•**sailles**
ver•sa•tile
ver•sa•**til**•i•ty
verse
ver•sion
ver•sus
ver•te•bra (sing.)
ver•te•brae (pl.)
ver•te•brate
ver•ti•cal
ver•y (sounds like
   "vary")
   She is very tall.
ves•sel
vest
vet
vet•er•an
vet•er•i•**nar**•i•an
vet•er•i•nar•y
ve•to
ve•toed
ve•toes
ve•to•ing

vi•a
vi•a•**bil**•i•ty
vi•a•ble
vi•a•duct
vi•brant
vi•brate
vi•brat•ing
vi•**bra**•tion
vice (sounds like
   "vise")
   Cheating is a vice.

Viking

vice pres•i•dent
vice ver•sa
vi•**cin**•i•ties
vi•**cin**•i•ty
vi•cious
vic•tim
vic•tim•i•**za**•tion

vic•tim•ize
vic•tim•iz•ing
vic•tor
vic•to•ries
vic•**to**•ri•ous
vic•to•ry
vid•e•o
vid•e•o•cas•**sette**
vid•e•o•tape
vie
vied
Vi•**en**•na
Vi•et•**nam**
view
view•point
vig•i•lance
vig•i•lant
vig•or
vig•or•ous
Vi•king
vile
vil•la
vil•lage
vil•lag•er
vil•lain
vil•lain•ous
vil•lain•y
vin•**dic**•tive
vin•**dic**•tive•ness
vine
vin•e•gar
vine•yard
vin•tage
vi•nyl

vi•o•la

vi•o•late

vi•o•lat•ing

vi•o•la•tion

vi•o•la•tor

vi•o•lence

vi•o•lent

vi•o•let

vi•o•lin

vi•per

Vir•gin•ia

vir•tu•al•ly

vir•tu•al re•al•i•ty

vir•tue

vir•tu•o•so

vir•tu•ous

vi•rus

vi•sa

vise (sounds like "vice")

Put the wood in a vise before you saw it.

vis•i•bil•i•ty

vis•i•ble

vis•i•bly

vi•sion

vis•it

vis•it•or

vi•sor

vis•ta

vis•u•al

vi•su•a•li•za•tion

vi•su•a•lize

vi•tal

vi•tal•i•ty

vi•ta•min

vi•va•cious

viv•id

viv•id•ness

vo•cab•u•lar•ies

vo•cab•u•lar•y

vo•cal

vo•cal cords

vo•cal•ist

vo•ca•tion

vo•cif•er•ous

vogue

voice

voice•print

voic•ing

void

vol•a•tile

vol•a•til•i•ty

vol•ca•no

vol•ca•noes (*or* vol•ca•nos)

vol•ley

vol•ley•ball

volt

volt•age

vol•ume

vo•lu•mi•nous

vol•un•tar•y

vol•un•teer

vom•it

vote

vow

vow•el

voy•age

voy•ager

vul•gar

vul•ner•a•bil•i•ty

vul•ner•a•ble

vul•ture

vy•ing

wack•i•er

wack•i•est

wack•i•ness

wack•y

wad

wad•dle

wad•dling

wade

wad•er

wad•ing

wa•fer

waf•fle

waf•fling

waft

wag

wage

wa•ger

wagged

wag•ging

wag•ing

wag•on

waif

wail (sounds like "whale")

The baby will wail when her mother leaves.

waist (sounds like "waste")

He has a 32-inch waist.

wait (sounds like "weight")

Wait for me!

wait•er

wait•ress

waive (sounds like "wave")

Did he waive his right to a lawyer?

walrus

waiv•ing

wake

wak•ing

walk

walk•er

walk•ie-talk•ie

walk•o•ver

walk•way

wall

wal•la•bies

wal•la•by

wal•let

wal•lop

wal•low

wall•pa•per

wal•nut

wal•rus

waltz

wam•pum

wand

wan•der

wane

wan•gle

wan•gling

wan•ing

want

war

war•ble

war•bler

ward

war•den

ward•robe

ware•house

wares (sounds like "wears")

There are wonderful wares to purchase here.

war•fare

war•i•ly

war•like

warm

warm-blood•ed

warm•er

warm•est

warmth

warn (sounds like "worn")

Warn him of the danger.

warp

war•rant

war•ran•ty

war•ri•or

war•ship

wart

war•y

was

wash

wash•a•ble

wash•er

wash•ing ma•chine

Wash•ing•ton

was•n't

wasp

waste (sounds like "waist")

What a waste of time!

waste•bas•ket

wast•ed

waste•ful

waste•ful•ness

waste•land

wast•ing

watch

watch•dog

watch•ful

watch•ful•ness

wa•ter

wa•ter•col•or

wa•ter•cool•er

wa•ter•cress

wa•ter•fall

wa•ter•front

wa•ter•ing

wa•ter•logged

wa•ter•mark

wa•ter•mel•on

watermelon

wa•ter **pis**•tol

wa•ter•proof

wa•ter•shed

wa•ter-**ski**

wa•ter-**skied**

wa•ter-**ski**•er

wa•ter•ski•ing

wa•ter•tight

wa•ter•way

wa•ter•wheel

wa•ter•works

watt

wave (sounds like "waive")

Surfers love a huge wave.

wave•length

wa•ver

wav•ing

wav•y

wax

wax•y

way (sounds like "weigh")

Which way to the elephant house, please?

we (sounds like "wee")

We are happy to be here.

weak (sounds like "week")

She was weak after her illness.

weak•en

weak•ling

weak•ness

wealth

wealth•i•er

wealth•i•est

wealth•y

wean

weap·on

weap·on·ry

wear

wear·i·er

wear·i·est

wear·i·ly

wear·i·ness

wears (sounds like "wares")

He wears green every Friday.

wea·ry

wea·sel

weath·er (sounds like "whether")

I like cold weather.

weath·er-beat·en

weath·er·ize

weath·er **vane**

weave (sounds like "we've")

She could weave a whole tapestry.

weav·er

weav·ing

web

web-**foot**·ed

wed

we'd (sounds like "weed")

We'd better be going now.

wed·ded

wed·ding

wedge

Wed·nes·day

wee (sounds like "we")

The wee man was an elf.

weed (sounds like "we'd")

I'll pluck that weed out of my garden.

week (sounds like "weak")

Next week I'm going to Texas.

week·day

week·end

week·lies

week·ly

weep

wee·vil

weigh (sounds like "way")

I weigh more than I did when I was born.

weighed

weight (sounds like "wait")

The weight of those boxes can break the table.

weight·less

weight lift·er

weird

weird·o

weird·os

wel·come

wel·com·ing

weld

weld·er

wel·fare

well

we'll (sounds like "wheel")

We'll have to see about that.

well-**bal**·anced

well-be·**haved**

well-**be**·ing

well-known

well-off

went

were (sounds like "whir")

They were there yesterday.

we're

weren't

west

west·er·ly

west·ern

West In·dies

West Vir·**gin**·ia

west·ward

wet

wet·land

wet·ter

wet·test

we've (sounds like "weave")

We've spoken about this before.

whack

whale (sounds like "wail")

We went on a whale-watching cruise.

whal•er

whal•ing

wharf

what

what•**ev**•er

what's

wheat

wheel (sounds like "we'll")

The wheel on my bike fell off.

wheel•bar•row

wheel•chair

wheel•ie

wheeze

wheez•ing

wheez•y

whelk

when

when•**ev**•er

where

where•a•bouts

where•**as**

wher•**ev**•er

wheth•er (sounds like "weather")

We will leave at 9 AM whether you're ready or not.

whew

which (sounds like "witch")

Which hat will you wear today?

whiff

while

whim

whim•per

whine

whin•er

whin•ing

whin•nied

whin•nies

whin•ny

whip

whipped

whip•ping

whip•poor•will

whir (sounds like "were")

The whir of the fan was loud.

whirl

whirl•pool

whirl•wind

whirred

whir•ring

whisk

whisk•er

whis•key

whis•per

whis•tle

whis•tling

white

White House

white•wash

whit•tle

whit•tling

whiz (*or* **whizz**)

whizzed

who

whoa

who'd

who•**ev**•er

whole (sounds like "hole")

You ate the whole pie yourself?

whole•sale

whole•sal•er

whole•some

who'll

whol•ly (sounds like "holy")

I am wholly satisfied with your grade.

whom

whom•**ev**•er

whoop

whoop•ing **cough**

whoop•ing **crane**

who's (sounds like "whose")

Who's responsible for this mess?

whose (sounds like "who's")

Whose skates are these?

why
wick
wick·ed
wick·er
wide
wide·spread
wid·ow
wid·ow·er
width
wife
wig
wig·gle
wig·gler
wig·gling
wild
wild·cat
wil·der·ness
wild·flow·er
wild·life
will
will·ful
will·ful·ness
will·ing
will·ing·ness
wil·low
wilt
wimp
win
wind (rhymes with "skinned")

Do you feel the wind?

wind (rhymes with "kind")

It's time to wind down this game.

wind-chill **fac**·tor
wind·mill

windmill

win·dow
win·dow·pane
win·dow-shop·ping
wind·pipe
wind·shear
wind·shield
wind·surf·er
wind·surf·ing
wind·swept
wind·y
wine
wing
wing·span
wink
win·ner

win·ning
win·ter
win·ter·green
win·ter·time
win·try
wipe
wip·ing
wire
wir·ing
wir·y
Wis·**con**·sin
wis·dom
wise
wish
wish·bone
wish·es
wisp
wis·**te**·ri·a
wist·ful
wit
witch (sounds like "which")

The witch rode a broomstick.

with
with·**draw**
with·**draw**·al
with·**drawn**
with·er
with·**hold**
with·**in**
with·**out**
with·**stand**
with·**stood**

wit•ness

wit•ty

wives

wiz•ard

wiz•ar•dry

wob•ble

wob•bling

wob•bly

woe

wok

woke

wolf

wol•ver•ine

wolves

wom•an

wom•an•hood

womb

wom•bat

wom•en

won (sounds like "one")

We won the championship!

won•der

won•der•ful

won't

wood (sounds like "would")

Wood is an excellent building material.

wood•chuck

wood•en

wood•land

wood•peck•er

(worm)

wood•wind

wood•work

wool

wool•en

word

word•ing

word proc•ess•ing

word proc•es•sor

word•y

wore

work

work•a•ble

work•a•hol•ic

work•bench

work•book

work•er

work•man

work•man•ship

work•out

work•shop

work•sta•tion

world

World War I

World War II

world•wide

worm

worn (sounds like "warn")

This shirt is so worn it has holes in it.

worn-out

wor•ried

wor•ries

wor•ry

wor•ry•ing

worse

wor•ship

worst

worth

worth•less

worth•while

wor•thy

would (sounds like "wood")

I would like you to come.

would•n't

wound (rhymes with "crooned")

The doctor bandaged his wound.

wound (rhymes with "round")

He wound the clock every day.

wove

wran•gle

wran•gler

wran•gling

wrap (sounds like "rap")

Will you wrap my package?

wrapped

wrap•per

wrap•ping

wrath

wreak (sounds like "reek")

This twister will wreak havoc on the town.

wreath

wreck

wreck•age

wren

wrench

wres•tle

wres•tler

wres•tling

wretch

wretch•ed

wrig•gle

wrig•gling

wring (sounds like "ring")

Wring all the water out of your bathing suit.

wrin•kle

wrin•kling

wrist

wrist•watch

write (sounds like "right")

I'll write you every day.

writ•er

writ•ing

writ•ten

wrong

wrong•do•ing

wrote (sounds like "rote")

Shakespeare wrote great plays.

wrung

wry (sounds like "rye")

He has a wry sense of humor.

Wy•**om**•ing

Xe•rox

X ray (n.)

X-ray (adj. and v.)

xy•lo•phone

Y

yacht
yacht•ing
yak
yam
yank
Yan•kee
yap
yapped
yap•ping
yard
yard•stick
yar•mul•ke
yarn
yawn
year
year•book
year•ling
yearn
yeast
yell
yel•low
yel•low jack•et
Yel•low•stone
yelp
yen
yes
yes•ter•day
yet
Yid•dish
yield
yip

yipped
yip•ping
yo
yo•del
yo•ga
yo•gi
yo•gurt
yoke (sounds like "yolk")
The oxen shared a yoke.
yolk (sounds like "yoke")
Eat your egg yolk.
Yom **Kip**•pur
also pronounced
Yom Kip•**pur**
yon•der

yo-yo

Yo•**sem**•i•te
you (sounds like "ewe")
I'm glad to meet you.
you'd
you'll (sounds like "Yule")
You'll see.
young
young•ster
your (sounds like "you're")
Here is your change.
you're (sounds like "your")
You're very welcome.
yours
your•self
your•selves
youth
you've
yowl
yo-yo
Yu•kon
Yule (sounds like "you'll")
I love the Yule season.
Yule•tide
yup•pies
yup•py

za•ny
zap
zapped
zap•ping
zeal
zeal•ot
zeal•ous
ze•bra
ze•nith
zeph•yr
zep•pe•lin
ze•ro
ze•ros (*or* ze•roes)
zest
zest•ful
Zeus
zig•zag
zig•zagged
zilch

zinc
zin•ni•a
Zi•on•ism
Zi•on•ist
zip
zip code (*or* ZIP code)

zebra

zipped
zip•per
zip•ping
zip•py
zir•**co**•ni•um
zith•er
zo•di•ac
zom•bie
zone
zon•ing
zoo
zo•o•**log**•i•cal
zo•**ol**•o•gist
zo•**ol**•o•gy
zoom
zuc•**chi**•ni
Zu•lu
Zu•ni
Zu•rich

Misspeller's Dictionary

Looking up a word can be really difficult if you get the first, or initial, sound wrong. Here are over 600 words with tricky beginnings. The word in the left column is the wrong spelling. Look in the right column for the right spelling.

Wrong Spelling	Right Spelling	Wrong Spelling	Right Spelling
chek	Czech	fizicist	physicist
chek	check	fizics	physics
chello	cello	fizique	physique
fantom	phantom	fizishun	physician
farmacist	pharmacist	flem	phlegm
farmacy	pharmacy	fobia	phobia
fase	phase	foenix	phoenix
faze	phase	fonetic	phonetic
feasant	pheasant	fonics	phonics
feenix	phoenix	fonograph	phonograph
fenomenal	phenomenal	fony	phony
fenomenon	phenomenon	fosforus	phosphorus
fezant	pheasant	fosphorus	phosphorus
filanthropic	philanthropic	fotocopy	photocopy
filanthropist	philanthropist	fotogenic	photogenic
filanthropy	philanthropy	fotografy	photography
filharmonic	philharmonic	fotograph	photograph
filodendron	philodendron	fotography	photography
filosopher	philosopher	fotojenic	photogenic
filosophy	philosophy	fraze	phrase
fizeek	physique	fysical	physical
fizical	physical	fysician	physician
fizician	physician	fysicist	physicist

Wrong Spelling	Right Spelling	Wrong Spelling	Right Spelling
fysics	physics	jenerous	generous
gage	gauge	jenesis	genesis
gastly	ghastly	jenetic	genetic
gerkin	gherkin	jenial	genial
getto	ghetto	jenie	genie
gliserin	glycerin	jenius	genius
gool	ghoul	jenocide	genocide
gost	ghost	jenra	genre
goul	ghoul	jenteel	genteel
heffer	heifer	jentile	gentile
hoo	who	jentle	gentle
hoom	whom	jentleman	gentleman
hoose	whose	jentry	gentry
hooz	whose	jenuine	genuine
jee	gee	jenus	genus
jeen	jean	jeodesic	geodesic
jee-wiz	gee-whiz	jeographic	geographic
jelatin	gelatin	jeography	geography
jem	gem	jeology	geology
jender	gender	jeolojic	geologic
jene	gene	jeometric	geometric
jeneologist	genealogist	jeometry	geometry
jeneology	genealogy	jeranium	geranium
jeneral	general	jerbil	gerbil
jeneralize	generalize	jeriatric	geriatric
jenerate	generate	jerm	germ
jeneration	generation	Jerman	German
jenerator	generator	jerminate	germinate
jenerosity	generosity	jerund	gerund

Wrong Spelling	Right Spelling	Wrong Spelling	Right Spelling
jesticulate	gesticulate	kache	cache
jesture	gesture	kackle	cackle
jiant	giant	kactus	cactus
jibber	gibber	kadet	cadet
jibberish	gibberish	kaf	calf
jibe	gibe	kafay	café
jigantic	gigantic	kaffeine	caffeine
jim	gym	kage	cage
jimnast	gymnast	kalf	calf
jimnastic	gymnastic	kalico	calico
jinger	ginger	kalipso	calypso
jinseng	ginseng	kall	call
jipsy	gypsy	kalligraphy	calligraphy
jiraffe	giraffe	kalliope	calliope
jist	gist	kalm	calm
jym	gym	kalorie	calorie
jymnasium	gymnasium	kalypso	calypso
jymnast	gymnast	kamel	camel
jymnastic	gymnastic	kamoflaje	camouflage
jypsum	gypsum	kampain	campaign
jypsy	gypsy	kampus	campus
jyrate	gyrate	Kanada	Canada
jyroscope	gyroscope	kanary	canary
kab	cab	kancel	cancel
kabbage	cabbage	kandelabra	candelabra
kabin	cabin	kandid	candid
kabinet	cabinet	kandidate	candidate
kable	cable	kandle	candle
kaboose	caboose	kandy	candy

Wrong Spelling	Right Spelling	Wrong Spelling	Right Spelling
kanine	canine	kardigan	cardigan
kanister	canister	kardinal	cardinal
kanker	canker	kardiograph	cardiograph
kannibal	cannibal	kare	care
kannon	cannon	kareer	career
kanoe	canoe	kareful	careful
kanoo	canoe	karess	caress
kanopy	canopy	karibou	caribou
kanser	cancer	karizma	charisma
kantalope	cantaloupe	karnation	carnation
kanteen	canteen	karnivore	carnivore
kantor	cantor	karpenter	carpenter
kanvas	canvas	karpet	carpet
kanyon	canyon	karrige	carriage
kaos	chaos	karrot	carrot
kapital	capital	kartilage	cartilage
kapitol	capitol	kartoon	cartoon
kapshun	caption	kartridge	cartridge
kapsule	capsule	karve	carve
kaptain	captain	kascade	cascade
kaption	caption	kashew	cashew
kaptivate	captivate	kashier	cashier
kaptive	captive	kaskade	cascade
kapture	capture	kasket	casket
kar	car	kasm	chasm
karacter	character	kassette	cassette
karamel	caramel	kastanets	castanets
karavan	caravan	kastle	castle
karbon	carbon	kasual	casual

Wrong Spelling	Right Spelling	Wrong Spelling	Right Spelling
katacomb	catacomb	koral	choral
katalog	catalog	korale	chorale
katalyst	catalyst	kord	chord
katapult	catapult	kord	cord
katastrophe	catastrophe	koreography	choreography
katch	catch	korus	chorus
kategory	category	krab	crab
katerpillar	caterpillar	kracker	cracker
kattle	cattle	kradle	cradle
kaucus	caucus	kraft	craft
kaught	caught	krag	crag
kauliflower	cauliflower	kramp	cramp
kauk	caulk	kranberry	cranberry
kaushon	caution	krane	crane
kavalcade	cavalcade	kranium	cranium
kavalier	cavalier	krank	crank
kavalry	cavalry	kranny	cranny
kavern	cavern	krape	crepe
kavity	cavity	krash	crash
kawk	caulk	krate	crate
kawt	caught	krater	crater
kazm	chasm	krave	crave
kemical	chemical	krawl	crawl
kemist	chemist	krawssant	croissant
kemistry	chemistry	krayon	crayon
klorine	chlorine	krazy	crazy
kloroform	chloroform	kreak	creak
klorophyll	chlorophyll	kreak	creek
kolera	cholera	kream	cream

Wrong Spelling	Right Spelling	Wrong Spelling	Right Spelling
krease	crease	krome	chrome
kreate	create	kromium	chromium
kredit	credit	kromosome	chromosome
kreek	creek	kronic	chronic
kreek	creak	kronicle	chronicle
kreem	cream	kronology	chronology
kreep	creep	krooked	crooked
krescent	crescent	krooze	cruise
kreviss	crevice	krop	crop
krew	crew	kross	cross
kricket	cricket	krouch	crouch
kriminal	criminal	krow	crow
kringe	cringe	krowd	crowd
kripple	cripple	krown	crown
kript	crypt	krucial	crucial
krisis	crisis	krucifix	crucifix
Krismas	Christmas	krude	crude
krisp	crisp	kruel	cruel
krissen	christen	kruise	cruise
krisskross	crisscross	krum	crumb
Krissmass	Christmas	krumble	crumble
kritic	critic	krumple	crumple
kriticism	criticism	krunch	crunch
kriticize	criticize	krusade	crusade
krochety	crotchety	krushal	crucial
krockery	crockery	krustacean	crustacean
krocodile	crocodile	krusty	crusty
krocus	crocus	kruze	cruise
kroissant	croissant	kry	cry

217

Wrong Spelling	Right Spelling	Wrong Spelling	Right Spelling
krypt	crypt	kwire	choir
krysalis	chrysalis	kwit	quit
krystal	crystal	kwite	quite
kwack	quack	kwivver	quiver
kwail	quail	kwiz	quiz
kwaint	quaint	kwoshunt	quotient
kwake	quake	kwota	quota
kwalify	qualify	kwote	quote
kwality	quality	kwotient	quotient
kwantity	quantity	nack	knack
kwarrel	quarrel	napsack	knapsack
kwarry	quarry	narl	gnarl
kwart	quart	nash	gnash
kwarter	quarter	nat	gnat
kwartz	quartz	nave	knave
kwash	quash	naw	gnaw
kween	queen	nead	knead
kweer	queer	nead	need
kweezy	queasy	nee	knee
kwell	quell	neel	kneel
kwench	quench	nell	knell
kwest	quest	nickerbockers	knickerbockers
kwestion	question	nife	knife
kwibble	quibble	nite	knight
kwick	quick	nite	night
kwiet	quiet	nob	knob
kwill	quill	nock	knock
kwilt	quilt	nockwurst	knockwurst
kwip	quip	noe	know

Wrong Spelling	Right Spelling	Wrong Spelling	Right Spelling
noe	no	rowt	rote
noll	knoll	salm	psalm
nome	gnome	sayder	seder
noo	gnu	sease	cease
nothole	knothole	seedar	cedar
notty	knotty	seenic	scenic
nowledge	knowledge	seiling	ceiling
nown	known	selebrate	celebrate
nu	gnu	selebrity	celebrity
nuckle	knuckle	selery	celery
numatic	pneumatic	selestial	celestial
numonia	pneumonia	sellar	cellar
onest	honest	sellar	seller
phantasy	fantasy	sellophane	cellophane
rack	wrack	sellular	cellular
rangle	wrangle	selluloid	celluloid
reath	wreath	sement	cement
reched	wretched	sene	scene
reck	wreck	sene	seen
reckage	wreckage	senery	scenery
reeth	wreath	sensur	censor
rench	wrench	sensur	sensor
restle	wrestle	sensorship	censorship
riggle	wriggle	sent	cent
rinkle	wrinkle	sent	scent
rist	wrist	sentennial	centennial
rite	write	senter	center
rong	wrong	sentigrade	centigrade
rowt	wrote	sentimeter	centimeter

Wrong Spelling	Right Spelling	Wrong Spelling	Right Spelling
sentipede	centipede	shuneel	chenille
sentral	central	shure	sure
sentrifugal	centrifugal	shute	chute
sentury	century	sider	cider
septer	scepter	sience	science
seramic	ceramic	sifer	cipher
sereal	cereal	sigar	cigar
seremony	ceremony	sigarette	cigarette
sertain	certain	silinder	cylinder
sertificate	certificate	sinch	cinch
sertify	certify	sinder	cinder
seudonym	pseudonym	sinema	cinema
shagrin	chagrin	sinic	cynic
shalay	chalet	sinnamon	cinnamon
shammy	chamois	sintillate	scintillate
shampain	champagne	sipher	cipher
shandelier	chandelier	sircle	circle
sharade	charade	sirculate	circulate
sharlatan	charlatan	sircumference	circumference
shateau	chateau	sircus	circus
shatoe	chateau	sissors	scissors
sheek	chic	sist	cyst
sheek	sheikh	sitadel	citadel
shef	chef	sitizen	citizen
shiffon	chiffon	sitrus	citrus
shivalry	chivalry	sivic	civic
showfer	chauffeur	sivil	civil
showvinist	chauvinist	sivilian	civilian
shugar	sugar	sivilization	civilization

Wrong Spelling	Right Spelling	Wrong Spelling	Right Spelling
sivilize	civilize	skorch	scorch
sizzors	scissors	skore	score
skab	scab	skorn	scorn
skald	scold	skotch	scotch
skale	scale	skoundrel	scoundrel
skallion	scallion	skout	scout
skallop	scallop	skowl	scowl
skalp	scalp	skowndrel	scoundrel
skamper	scamper	skraggly	scraggly
skan	scan	skram	scram
skandal	scandal	skramble	scramble
skant	scant	skrap	scrap
skar	scar	skrape	scrape
skarce	scarce	skratch	scratch
skare	scare	skrawl	scrawl
skarf	scarf	skrawny	scrawny
skary	scary	skream	scream
skatter	scatter	skreech	screech
skavenge	scavenge	skreen	screen
skedule	schedule	skrew	screw
skeem	scheme	skribble	scribble
skitzophrenic	schizophrenic	skrimmage	scrimmage
skoff	scoff	skript	script
skolar	scholar	skripture	scripture
skolastic	scholastic	skroll	scroll
skool	school	skrounge	scrounge
skooner	schooner	skrub	scrub
skoop	scoop	skruffy	scruffy
skooter	scooter	skruple	scruple

Wrong Spelling	Right Spelling	Wrong Spelling	Right Spelling
skrutinize	scrutinize	skwint	squint
skuba	scuba	skwire	squire
skuff	scuff	skwirm	squirm
skullery	scullery	skwirrel	squirrel
skulpt	sculpt	skwirt	squirt
skulpture	sculpture	skwish	squish
skum	scum	soodonim	pseudonym
skwabble	squabble	sychiatrist	psychiatrist
skwad	squad	sychic	psychic
skwadron	squadron	sychology	psychology
skwak	squawk	sycle	cycle
skwall	squall	syclist	cyclist
skwalor	squalor	syclone	cyclone
skwander	squander	syclorama	cyclorama
skware	square	sylinder	cylinder
skwash	squash	symbal	cymbal
skwat	squat	synic	cynic
skwaw	squaw	sypress	cypress
skweak	squeak	syst	cyst
skweal	squeal	sythe	scythe
skweamish	squeamish	terodactyl	pterodactyl
skweek	squeak	tomaine	ptomaine
skweel	squeal	wack	whack
skweemish	squeamish	wale	whale
skweez	squeeze	warf	wharf
skwelch	squelch	wat	what
skwib	squib	weat	wheat
skwid	squid	weaze	wheeze
skwiggle	squiggle	weel	wheel

Wrong Spelling	Right Spelling	Wrong Spelling	Right Spelling
weet	wheat	wiskey	whiskey
weeze	wheeze	wisper	whisper
wenn	when	wistle	whistle
Wenzday	Wednesday	wite	white
wether	weather	wittle	whittle
wether	whether	wiz	whiz
wich	which	woop	whoop
wich	witch	woosh	whoosh
wiff	whiff	wopper	whopper
wim	whim	wut	what
wimen	women	wy	why
wimper	whimper	yawt	yacht
wimsical	whimsical	zar	czar
wip	whip	zarina	czarina
wippersnapper	whippersnapper	zefer	zephyr
wippoorwill	whippoorwill	zenra	genre
wir	whir	Zerox	Xerox
wirlpool	whirlpool	zylophone	xylophone
wisker	whisker		

ABOUT THE AUTHOR

Marvin Terban's twenty books on the English language have been used to teach English as far away as China. He has won the Children's Choice award, and his *Scholastic Dictionary of Idioms* was named an American Bookseller "Pick of the Lists." A teacher of English, drama, and Latin, Mr. Terban lives in New York City.

PRAISE FOR OTHER SCHOLASTIC BOOKS BY MARVIN TERBAN:

Checking Your Grammar

Students will not have to wade through tedious or lengthy explanations to find what they need.... [This book is] attractive and so user-friendly that it can be read for fun.... *Grammar* illustrates the rules of proper grammar through nicely informal examples. The book also include chapters on sexist language, spelling rules, homonyms, and easily confused and misused words....   —*ALA Booklist*

There's a lot of grammar packed into this compact volume, and anyone who doesn't have a computer with spell check and grammar check needs it. Each of the three sections ("Building Sentences," "Parts of Speech," and "Style and Usage") is preceded by a detailed table of contents. Many necessary examples are provided. There is an index, but the excellent tables of contents are more useful. All in all, a handy guide.   —*School Library Journal*

Scholastic Dictionary of Idioms

...Fascinating.... This unusual work will intrigue children and may whet their appetites for other explorations of language.   —*Kirkus Reviews*

Terban explains the meaning and origins (if known) of more than 600 idioms and proverbs in this intriguing book.... Terban has obviously done a great deal of research.... A good resource for teachers who discuss idioms in the classroom....
          —*ALA Booklist*

Reference tools may be a dime a dozen in this dog-eat-dog world, but here's a soup-to-nuts dictionary of colloquialisms that doesn't beat around the bush.... The sheer volume of examples...makes this an appealing browse as well as a useful (and perhaps unique) resource for kids baffled by the intricacies of the English language.
          —*The Bulletin of the Center for Children's Books*